# DOWSING AND ARCHAEOLOGY

Gary '83

Olson

# DOWSING
# AND ARCHAEOLOGY

An anthology from the Journal of the British Society of Dowsers

## Edited by Tom Graves

TURNSTONE BOOKS
Wellingborough, Northamptonshire

This anthology first published 1980

© jointly British Society of Dowsers and contributory authors 1980


ISBN  0 85500 109 7 (hardback)
      0 85500 110 0 (paperback)

Prepared by Wordsmith Graphics, Street

Printed and bound in Great Britain by
Weatherby Woolnough, Wellingborough
Northamptonshire.

# Contents

# Editor's Introduction

The art of the dowser has many applications. This selection of articles from the *Journal of the British Society of Dowsers* shows one of them, its use in archaeological research; or rather, its use in two quite different approaches to archaeology. The first part of the anthology shows the scope of dowsing in conventional archaeological research, particularly its use as a non-destructive tool to point out suitable sites for excavation. The second part (from page 40 onwards) shows how dowsers have developed an archaeology of their own, based on correlations between ancient sites and 'earth energies' from underground water and the like.

The articles span nearly fifty years: the first article here was printed in the first issue of the *Journal* in 1933. All the articles are practical rather than theoretical, and most give full details of the sites discussed, so that others may check the work described. Many of the articles do assume a basic knowledge of dowsing practice of the time: for older techniques, see Mermet's *Radiesthesia* (Stuart and Watkins, 1959), while the current techniques and approaches are described in Scott-Elliot's *Dowsing — One Man's Way* (Spearman, 1976) and my own *Dowsing — Techniques and Applications* (Turnstone, 1976). In most cases the articles in this anthology are reproduced exactly as they appeared in the *Journal*; the only exceptions are three of Guy Underwood's lengthier articles, from which some digressions and descriptive references to other articles in this anthology have been removed.

I do feel that some comment on the articles is necessary: among other reasons, in order to place them within the current context of archaeological dowsing. In some cases, too, the opinions held by the authors are disputed by others, or are considered out of date — even by the authors themselves. Sometimes the methods described seem bizarre, but those methods, however 'unscientific', were those which were found to work by the person doing the work at the time. There are no set methods in dowsing — the results alone are the important matter.

A good case in point can be seen in the first article: the comment "using a green and white pendulum — for it was raining". Colour responses were considered to be an essential part of dowsing at the time — as described in detail in Mermet's *Radiesthesia* — but is now regarded as a rather minor aspect of dowsing. The article is followed by an editorial comment and a follow-up (using slightly different techniques) of nearly a quarter of a century later. They all deal with the dowser's classic problem of water supply, this time in a classic setting.

The next two pieces, both describing sites in Kensington in west London, give good examples of the dowser's ability to pick out a given range of information from amongst the jumble of layer upon layer of foundations and buildings in a long-developed area. The first article gives a very clear description of the procedure, leading to (literally) concrete evidence; the barracks, incidentally, are still standing, so the "more detailed excavation" seems unlikely for some time to come!

Latham's lecture/article which follows (pages 15–27) shows typical attitudes and activities in the early 1960s, while the extract from Major-General Scott-Elliot's article shows the same for the early '70s. Much is unchanged; the main difference is the routine use of map-dowsing as a preliminary for field-work, as discussed in the later article.

Plummer's mid-'70s work on Roman roads in his own part of north-east England describes the now-standard sequence for dowsing in 'conventional' archaeology: library research, map dowsing, field dowsing, followed by selective digs wherever practicable — all well documented. This superb piece of research brings us to the end of the first part of the anthology.

The remainder shows the development of the dowsers' own view of archaeology, based on what many would describe as 'earth energies'. The staring points for this are Boothby's query on water supplies for ancient 'forts' (pages 40–41), and Smith's all-too-condensed lecture that presented a first detailed answer to that query. Both wrote before the War; both were respected men in their own fields — Smith particularly so, as an archaeologist with an international reputation; but both were old men at the time, and died with the decade. Their work was picked up after the War by Guy Underwood, who is probably the only well-known archaeological dowser. It may come as something of a surprise to readers of his *Pattern of the Past* (Pitman, 1969) that the real work for the book was done twenty years before its publication.

I make no excuse for including so much of Underwood's work in this anthology. He was a prolific writer and researcher on several dowsing topics; his writings in the *Journal* on his archaeological work alone total little less than those of all the other writers put together. His work is well documented and well illustrated; one article gives a clear description of survey technique (pages 65–66) which is still valid today. The work shown here is a good example of the development of a theory through practice, even if it is, as I feel, a theory which is one-sided and misses several key points. Others had their doubts at the time, too: see the rather brusque comments which the then editor, Colonel Bell, inserted at the end of Underwood's last two articles (pages 105 and 111). Those comments are probably the main reason why Underwood's final work, far more dogmatic than the exploratory work here, was left unpublished until some years after his death.

Underwood's theories may be invalid, but his observations were accurate — as is pointed out by the two brief notes on old churches, by Lamb and Langdon, which follow it — and it stands as the base for much current research by dowsers. Leonard's work at Moulton shows a fairly common approach of the present time, combining the meticulous attention to detail of Plummer's work on Roman roads with a part-mystical variant of Underwood's research and a ley-hunter's attitude to 'natural earth energies'.

Leonard's piece ends the anthology. Descriptions of some other current archaeological dowsing, and interpretations of that work, can be found in a number of recent books, including Scott-Elliot's *Dowsing — One Man's Way*, Francis Hitching's *Earth Magic* (Cassell, 1976) and my own *Needles of Stone* (Turnstone, 1978). But these books, and the writers in this anthology, can only point out ways and means; much research remains to be done along the lines that they show.

# Series Editor's Note

This is the first of a planned series of anthologies from the *Journal of the British Society of Dowsers,* presenting a number of themes in dowsing to a wider audience. These books are prepared by direct photographic reproduction from the *Journal*, and the print quality of the original does vary in places, as can be expected in a Journal whose issues span nearly fifty years and several changes of printer and printing process. We feel, however, that this is more than compensated for by the quality of the articles!

The opinions presented in the articles in this anthology are not necessarily held by the British Society of Dowsers, or currently even by their authors, as their opinions may have changed with later developments and the passing of time. Some articles have been included more for their historical importance or interest than for their relevance to current dowsing theory or practice.

The British Society of Dowsers was founded in 1933 as a reference point for people interested in all forms of dowsing, whether practical or theoretical. The current Secretary is Mr. Michael Rust, of Court Lodge Farm, Hastingleigh, Ashford, Kent, from whom details of the *Journal* and membership of the Society may be obtained.

# THE ROMAN VILLA AT BIGNOR

*'Campana' (Captain W.H. Trinder) and Editorial*

FOR over a hundred years the Roman Villa at Bignor, a few yards west of Stane Street, the highway between London and Chichester (Regnum), has attracted the attention of all who are interested in the Roman occupation of this country. The foundations of many of the buildings have been exposed, and several fine mosaics are still preserved in their original position. In the atrium on the north side of the inner court the masonry of a fountain can still be seen, and the bath at the south east corner of the court is in a fair state of preservation. There is, however, no trace of the source from which the members of the Roman household obtained their supply of water.

With the object of solving this problem, three representatives of the B.S.D. visited the villa on Saturday, May 27th. One of them is a skilled amateur who has studied the methods of the well-known French dowser, Monsieur Henri Mager—methods which are based on the selective effect of colours.

Using a green and white pendulum—for it was raining—and working from the shelter of the buildings on the north side of what was once the inner court, the operator quickly obtained an intersection in the neighbourhood of the old tree stump, on the south slope of the rise to the north-east of the Villa. Proceeding to the spot he verified his observation by means of a whalebone divining rod (or detector) of the appropriate colour, green, which indicated a stream at a depth of about 14 ft. There were also indications of a flow of water to the immediate north of the atrium.

Proceeding then to the bath at the south-east corner of the court, the operator, using a detector of the colour suitable for lead, a mixture of red and grey, obtained clear indications of that metal at the north-west corner of the bath where a tree is now standing. Walking round the crops which are growing in the inner court, he again obtained indications of lead at a depth of 4 to 5 ft. on the north side.

No doubt in Roman times the spring flowed out at the surface, and the site of the Villa was selected on the slope below, where a head of water would be available. The Romans had no means of conducting water under pressure, as their only pipes were of earthenware or lead, so it was essential that the source of water should be close to the buildings, and preferably at a higher level.

---

The above article has been reproduced from *B.S.D.J.*, I, 1, p. 18, as the event therein described might be of special interest to the enthusiastic water diviner next summer. The dowser mentioned is the late Captain W. H. Trinder, but no opportunity has hitherto occurred of verifying his observations. However, during 1959 further excavations on the site of the Villa were carried out by Mr. Sheppard Frere, F.S.A., and amongst his discoveries was a lead pipe on the north side of the Villa, apparently in the same position as that indicated by Captain Trinder. It would be very interesting if some other experienced dowser could verify the possible existence of a spring which 1,600 years ago reached the surface, but no longer does so.

Bignor is about five miles south of Petworth in Sussex. The site of the Villa and the surrounding land belongs to Captain H. Tupper. The Villa can be visited from March 1st to October 31st, with the exception of Mondays, and a guide is always available. Any competent dowser proposing to try to locate the source of the supply used by the Romans, should inform Captain Tupper beforehand, as he would like to be present. His address is : Roman Pavement, Bignor, Pulborough, Sussex. Telephone Sutton 202.—EDITOR.

# BIGNOR VILLA WATER SUPPLY
*Major C.A. Pogson*

Reproduced from *Sussex Notes and Queries*, Vol. XV, p. 192, published by the Sussex Archaeological Society.

For 149 years the source of the Villa's water supply, that important aspect of Roman achievement, has defied detection and still remains a mystery. In the absence of something concrete in the shape of a chance " find " the matter appears to have been dismissed without adequate consideration. It has been propounded that there was a superficial spring, now extinct, there was a piped supply or a well, but to the best of my knowledge the pros and cons of these various alternatives have not been compared. This particular problem has always been of special interest to me and so it was with the greatest pleasure that I availed myself of a suggestion by Captain H. Tupper to carry out a survey by dowsing with the hope that this method might perhaps produce a solution of the problem or at least throw some light on the matter.

Two of four possible means of obtaining water can, without doubt, be eliminated so far as the requirements of the Villa in its heyday are concerned. These are rain storage and transport

6

from a surface source in containers by man and beast. The latter means may perhaps have been employed in the case of the earlier building or buildings when requirements would have been on a very modest scale. In any case they are not capable of proof.

There remain either (1) a method of boosting by means of a ram or pump from a surface source by a rising main pipe line to an elevated point and thence by pipe or leet to the Villa or (2) withdrawal by pump or wheel from an open well excavated on elevated ground thence direct by gravity feed to the Villa ; alternatively, by pumping to a required height and thence by gravity feed.

There is now but the one surface stream which flows through Bignor Park at the foot of the escarpment north of the Villa but having regard to certain geological and surface features this point called for further investigation. The existing stream has two heads, both issuing at heights slightly in excess of 200 O.D. in coombes near Glatting and Coldharbour farms, the one three quarters of a mile S.W. and the other seven-eighths mile S.S.W. of Bignor Church respectively. These coombes—a characteristic of the escarpments and dip slopes of the Downs mostly are related to the local joint system of the chalk which being lines of weakness have caused erosion to take place and result very often in steep valley heads on which a fluctuating water table exerts considerable effects and lavants (or bournes) break out in otherwise dry chalk valleys. These in turn can easily give rise to new channels and run-offs. Any more or less permanent rise in the water table would have the effect of producing new streams. There is ample evidence that the water table in the chalk in Roman times was considerably higher than it is nowadays for instance, to take a somewhat extreme example, it is said that the evidence afforded from Woodyates in Cranbourne Chase (Hants) tends to show that in late Roman times the bottom of a well could be no less than 60 feet above those of modern wells in the neighbourhood !

The two springs from the Glatting and Coldharbour coombes unite at the immediate west of Bignor, circle round below the village and turn east through Bignor Park. At the nearest point to, and to the immediate north of, the Villa the present height of this stream is about 70 O.D. or, in other words, about one hundred feet lower than the Villa and some 130 feet below the elevated ground situated at the north of the Villa.

A little further to the east of Coldharbour Farm there is another coombe which now produces a small spring, and it seems that on reaching the low ground its natural trend is not to join the other two streams but to turn east at once, parallel to and south of the Bignor—West Burton road. It follows then that between the two westerly streams and this most easterly one there exists a diminutive water parting. This small local folding may well be due to the effect of slip of the Greensand on the Gault, visible at

7

outcrop on the west of the village. Examination leads me to put forward the suggestion that the trend of the central stream is not what it used to be and that in Roman times its waters, in greater volume, might also have followed an eastern trend on the south of the Bignor—West Burton road. This stream would probably have been augmented by springs from other coombes now dry because the water table has dropped below their floors. Most of the water now seeps sub surface, but breaks as a spring near West Burton House which flows to the Arun. Owing to the effects of sub-aerial denudation the escarpment of the South Downs is continually receding southwards. While such movement is but small it can reasonably be postulated that 1700 years ago the position of the stream might have been further to the north than the present low ground.

From the foregoing it will be appreciated that my hypothesis is that in Roman days, in addition to the present stream in Bignor Park there was also one south of the present Bignor—West Burton road. This stream would have been closer and more convenient for the inhabitants of the original timber house who would use it for watering animals and taking away water for personal needs, but at some stage of the development of the Villa, when the question arose of a supply of water at the Villa and the decision was to obtain from surface sources, then the problem would at once have arisen whether to obtain from the north or the south. The former would necessitate a lift of some 130 feet, but once at the highest point the water would easily gravitate to the Villa : on the other hand use of the southern stream would involve pumping to some point to the north of the Villa to obtain a gravity feed. Even this would entail a lift of some 50-60 feet. I have some doubts whether either of these schemes would have been possible, in particular the former. Yet another possible scheme having a possibility of overcoming the lift problem would have been to impound the best of the spring heads and make use of a pipe rising main or perhaps an aqueduct ? I can scarcely visualise such a grandiose scheme for just a villa.

Now in all these cases it would have been necessary to use pipes. These could have been made of lead or tiles jacketed in concrete or composed of timber pipes joined by iron collars as found at Lindum (Lincoln) and Venta Icenorum (Caister-by-Norwich) respectively and other places. Had there been such lengths of piping it is reasonable to suppose that at least some remains would have been found, but with the exception of a short length of lead pipe nothing has come to light.

Search along the river bank in Bignor Park and in the low ground south of the Bignor—West Burton Road failed to reveal anything which might be connected with the above schemes. Having exhausted the various possibilities of provision from surface sources it remained to investigate the possibility of a well

8

supply. The Villa is situated on the southern slope of a fold of the Upper Greensand some 1½ miles long on an E.W. axis. The formation, in addition to various sands and marls, contains a kind of siliceous rottenstone—the malmstone—which can be quite a good water bearer in the form of isolated flows, in particular when the beds form a narrow escarpment in front of the Chalk hills. The highest point is slightly in excess of the 200ft. contour ; on the south, west and north it falls away to the 100ft. contour or less and on the east it slopes to the Arun. On its N.W. and N. flank it forms an escarpment, in places precipitous due to slip on the underlying Gault and Folkestone Beds. Examination of the scant exposures in the upper portions of the escarpment yielded no information. No springs present at surface and I was unable to find any indications of them in the nearby dip slope.

In order to obtain an overall picture of the underground sources in the immediate vicinity I carried out a survey by dowsing covering the area bounded by :—

| | |
|---|---|
| on the south | foot of the Downs |
| west | Bignor village |
| north | stream in Bignor Park |
| east | A N-S line midway between the Villa and Hadworth Farm |

In the whole of this area there exists only *one* underground flow, on a north-south trend, of any importance whatsoever. The course of this flow is of considerable and significant interest. It originates (i.e., has its catchment or gathering ground) in Bignor Park north of the escarpment, but south of the stream with which it has no connection: it pursues a more or less straight course under the escarpment—the field on top thereof—the field on the immediate north of the Villa *under the MUSEUM* ! Southwards, approaching the West Burton—Bignor road it loses intensity, is tending to split up and south of the road on the oncoming of the Lower Chalk it is no longer traceable. I estimate the depth of this flow in the vicinity of the Museum to be about 50ft. to 60ft.

While it is very possible that over the centuries the water table has fallen, nonetheless, having regard to the characteristics of the U.G. coupled with the problematic escarpment of Roman days I tend to the opinion that if indeed this flow was the source of the Villa's water supply then the well might have been 40ft.-50ft. deep. This figure is, of course, of speculative value.

I consider that the suggestion of a superficial spring, now defunct, must be ruled out—the malmstone and clay beds may be more or less horizontally bedded and the catchment area for superficial level would be too small. Spring-fed ponds such as found at the farm near Rockbourne Down (Hants.) and other sites, while perhaps suitable for those purposes, certainly would not be of value for such an important Villa as Bignor.

I consider that the well would have been sited on the line of this flow on a site up to some 200-300 feet north of the Villa. The advantage of such site would be that in addition to affording a gravity supply, separate leets could be led to the baths and the stock by starting with the one leet and then bifurcating to where required.

If the well had been in the precincts of the Villa some evidence of it would surely have been found at the time of the original excavation. The use of leets instead of piping would account for the lack of evidence of the supply system.

It would be of interest to know what quantity of water would probably have been required ?

I feel convinced that supply by well is the correct solution of the problem ; it remains to find the exact position of the well and I am hoping to tackle this problem when the ground is clear of crops.

Having regard to the significant fact, previously mentioned, that the Villa is located on the one and only flow west of Stane Street, I should like to think that its site was determined by the dictum of a Roman water diviner, which provides yet another answer to the question why the Villa was built so far from Stane Street.

I am grateful to Lord Viscount Mersey and to Captain H. Tupper for their co-operation in permitting me to carry out my researches on their properties.


# ARCHAEOLOGICAL DOWSING
## Editorial

In the *B.S.D. Journal* for March, 1941 (page 111), there was an all-too-brief reference to a remarkable example of successful dowsing for buried masonry performed in 1938 by one of our members, Mr. L. J. Latham, at Kensington Barracks. The note was compiled from a short notice in the *Observer* of February 11th, 1940, but a much more complete account, unknown to the Editor, had already appeared in the *Journal of the Royal Army Service Corps* for June, 1938, and it is from this more fundamental source that the following further information has been obtained.

Kensington Barracks are situated on a plot of War Department land at the south end of Church Street, Kensington, and on the east side. About ten yards beyond the north-east corner of the barrack site there formerly stood a brick conduit house, which was replaced years ago by a Victorian so-called replica.*

---

* An engraving of the interior of the original conduit house can be seen in Faulkner's *History and Antiquities of Kensington*, 1820.

The function of this conduit house appears to have been the control of a spring of water through culverts, one of which provided a supply of pure water to a house called Chelsea Palace, which had been built by Henry VIII as a residence for his children.

Exposed Double Concrete Wall. The Masonry above is probably contemporary with buildings of the " King's Royal Forcing Ground."

There had been an unconfirmed tradition that another culvert led to Kensington Palace, but this had always been officially discredited. Mr. Latham was, however, able to confirm, after careful investigation, that such a culvert did actually exist, and has formed the opinion that the spring's output was tapped or supplemented by Nottingham House, as the Palace was called before Wren's alterations, for he traced a culvert of later construction than that leading to Chelsea Place, uniting the latter with a complicated network of brick waterways beneath the Palace.

It is interesting to note that in 1935, when a Victorian Jubilee Memorial was removed from the junction of High Street and Church Street, a sudden settlement revealed a broken portion of the Chelsea culvert which traversed this spot. Unfortunately, the work was sealed up with such dispatch that no proper archæological examination of the ancient masonry could be made. It appears, however, that the structure was man-size, of perfect Tudor brickwork, and wide-roofed in the Perpendicular style, except for a slightly pointed apex.

From this discovery Mr. Latham concluded that the culvert could hardly have avoided the site of Kensington Barracks to reach its destination at Chelsea Place, and to trace its exact path the use of the divining rod was suggested to him by (the then) Captain H. C. Davis, R.A.S.C.

Accordingly, Mr. Latham, using a sample of red brick, succeeded in tracing the course of the culvert for a considerable distance; but he found that instead of proceeding direct to the site of the Victorian Memorial the culvert made a peculiar diversion as if it were hugging the line of an unexpected obstacle, and then resumed its original alignment.

Mr. Latham then turned his attention to the unknown obstacle. He at once realised that it was not of brick, as no reaction was obtained when a brick sample was used. Samples of other material were tried with the same result, but reactions were obtained only when bare rods were used. The obstacle was traced step by step, and suggested a large rectangular network of foundations, about 190 by 210 feet in extent, with walls about four feet thick. Fortunately, a portion of the double outer wall ran below an unfloored basement at the south end of the eastern barrack block in which excavation was possible, and, in due course, at a depth of seventeen feet, a double concrete wall was actually uncovered.

In the course of excavation some interesting objects were brought to light in the shape of a testoon (shilling) of Henry VIII, a silver penny of James I, a bone knife-handle inscribed 'Clapham,' and pieces of oak timber.

As might be expected, there were traces of more than one period of occupation. Odd portions of ancient stonework and fragments of late Stewart brickwork, probably contemporaneous with the period when the site formed part of the kitchen garden of the adjacent palace, were unearthed. In the earliest available plan of the site, a map by Rogue of 1745, the plot is marked

"Kings Royal Forcing Ground," so the latest stratum may contain the remains of William III's conservatories.

The deflection of the culvert from the direct line clearly indicates that the existence of the concrete foundations was unknown to the Tudor engineers, as no one with an elementary knowledge of hydraulics would have intentionally introduced an unnecessary double bend into a conduit for water.

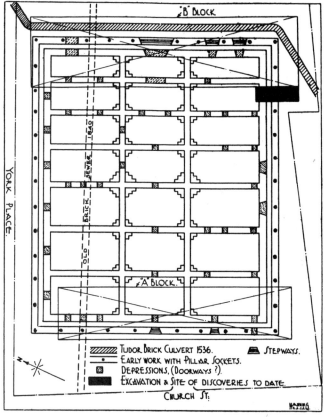

PLAN OF SUPPOSED ROMAN MASONRY AT KENSINGTON BARRACKS SHOWING DIVERSION OF TUDOR CULVERT AS REVEALED BY DOWSING.

There appears to have been difference of opinion regarding the date of the concrete foundation walls amongst the numerous archæological experts who examined them at the time. But the fact that the existence of these large obstructions was unknown

in the XVIth century, and that the use of concrete died out
with the decay of Roman civilisation in Britain and was not
resumed till comparatively recent times, is strong reason for
assuming that the remains are of Roman construction.

It is to be hoped that when the barracks, which before the war
were due for demolition, are pulled down, further areas of the
foundations will be revealed. It may then be possible to arrive
at a close idea of the date at which the walls were constructed
and the object for which the building was designed.


# UNDERGROUND PASSAGES IN KENSINGTON
*Catherine Ouless*


In Loftis's *Old Kensington* there is a description of Little
Campden House, built to accommodate the suite of Princess
Anne (afterwards Queen Anne) when she sent her little son,
the Duke of Gloucester, to live on Campden Hill for his health.
A passage was said to run from the house to Kensington Palace,
and when the Metropolitan Railway was made the tunnel from
Kensington High Street Station to Notting Hill Gate cut through
this passage. Mrs. Bruce, who lived in the house till the beginning
of the War, told me that the entrance to the passage was in her
cellars, but that she had had it bricked up. After the house was
destroyed by a fly-bomb in 1944, this entrance was exposed for
a short time, but immediately covered up. I traced the passage
with a pendulum and a rod as far as Holland Street.

Last year Mr. Latham, who made the interesting discovery
of Roman masonry under Kensington Barracks and has traced
various Tudor brick culverts in the neighbourhood, most kindly
came with me and confirmed what I had found. He traced
the passage as a 5ft. brick culvert with 14in. brick walls and a
vaulted roof. He calculated that it was about 14ft. down, that
is, about four or five feet below the cellars of the house.

In the account of the *B.S.D. Journal*, March, 1947, of Mr.
Latham's most interesting discoveries under Kensington Barracks
and of the Tudor culverts, he mentions that one supplied spring
water to Chelsea Place, built by Henry VIII as a summer
residence for his children. It would seem that the culvert, under
what was Little Campden House, situated higher up on Campden
Hill, was one of these Tudor waterways, especially as we traced
it down Church Walk at the back of St. Mary Abbots, instead
of in the direction of Kensington Palace.

# NOTICE OF ARCHAEOLOGICAL DIVINING
*L.J. Latham*

Mr. President, Ladies and Gentlemen, I thank you for the honour you do me in inviting me to present your Congress this year with a paper on one of my special studies in Radiesthesia. Some academic recognition of the possibilities of radiesthesia in this respect was adduced last Trinity Term when Oxford University's Archæological Faculty invited our Society to address it upon the subject. Inevitably, much of what I have to say to-day must embody the substance of what I said in my paper at the Ashmolean on that occasion. And as to my claim to discourse on this branch of divining ; it is twofold. Not least I count the fact that, myself an archæologist, I can recall with gratitude a hundred happy hours in its pursuit snatched from a busy life. But perhaps more specifically I have had the fortunate experience of employing divining itself in actual published archæological discovery. Indeed, I look back upon both field and surface researches across sites as widely scattered as Kensington and Colchester, Syria and South Arabia, and Egypt and Israel.

In a welter of written legend, tradition, mistranslation and even forgery, we can hardly base our study of the past solely upon the books with which we and our ancestors have surrounded ourselves. Only tools like the spade offer results tangible and exact enough for our purpose. The record thus recovered before our eyes, as it were, can be fairly readily interpreted by the expert into a proper historical context. Indeed, comparatively imperishable material, such as coins and other artifacts have normally a written message, and are frequently even dated by some era or other. Should there remain any last consideration to commend archæology to this Congress, it is that we are ourselves a most ancient and varied craft. We have roots, often shadowy and half-forgot, among all manner of peoples, lands and epochs. Let us therefore acknowledge that any study which investigates and perpetuates mankind's lore, his secrets, his beliefs and his traditions must command at once all our loyalty and service.

I think we may agree at the outset that there seem few among us indeed who have any experience of archæological prospecting by dowsing, fascinating as is this branch of our work. Not unnaturally, pride of place has more often been accorded to what we felt were the obvious needs in fields of minerals, water and medicine. It should therefore be stated at once that the same broad principles of operation apply here as in other dowser activities. For example, there are the same problems of fatigue, distortion, interference, autosuggestion and error cycles that dog the operator with such persistence in other types of prospecting.

15

Added, however, to these ordinary working troubles, we find in archæology an especially difficult complication. For herein, unlike the more substantial deposits of other *sorciers*, we are handling material that is often frail and destructible. Despite skilled and extreme care, the excavator can wreck vital evidence and disarrange otherwise readable strata. You will see at once that any method of detection that can guide the spade in these necessarily delicate delvings ought to command attention. But in this as in other fields of science, and let us confess not without reason, one often remains dubious as to the over-enthusiastic claims of the diviner. On the other hand, even were this ancient craft only partially effective, and then only under ideal conditions, it still justifies full field trials, provided always that these be carefully supervised. In practice in fact, no such extreme view against the dowser's claim is tenable, since the detectable matter of an archæological dig is as capable of discovery by a skilled and experienced worker as is water or any other specific. There is certainly enough evidence to show that more tolerance, opportunities and training would reduce our margin of error to the extent that we should prove quite useful members of any field team. But unless and until you are yourself a trained archæologist, be careful that you only indicate where excavation should take place. Too much damage can be done by unskilled hands for you yourself actually to meddle in the strata. Fortunately, in this class of prospecting, most deposits are not far from the surface, so that no error of judgment on your part can involve anyone in useless boring costs running into hundreds of pounds.

The average diviner called upon or permitted to guide such a dig would be well advised to first acquire from a friendly local museum curator fragments of the type of materials which he may expect to detect upon the site in question. Specimens of brick, Roman to Tudor in range, are obvious requisites. Antique shops and jewellers can often cheaply provide samples of ancient coins of the various metals, the period of which can be established by reference again to one's museum authority. From the same source too, can sometimes be obtained small fragments of the stone or the aggregates of which buried works are likely to be constructed. It should be here understood that these specimens are to be collected for use as field samples for the basic chemical element as expressed in the dowser's reflex. There is no sort of occult identity as between, for example, one coin and another. The diviner is merely reacting here to objects of different chemical composition, and it is precisely this difference in chemistry as between one portion of a deposit and another which is the diviners' sole concern. I think we may take it in passing that the doctrine of sample reading is now widely tested and is agreed among most of us. As indeed is also the concomitant doctrine of serial figures, as expressing a measurement of the relative dowsing strengths of the detectable elements. Even though we are not all in perfect agreement as to the position of such elements in our personally ascertained table of these strengths, we ought at least to master the accepted theory of samples and serials in so far as this is to affect the physics of our archæological work. The importance of this doctrine will be realised when it is recalled that archæological material rarely consists of a single element. The aggregates of ancient mortars for example are necessarily conglomerate in admixture, and can range from Roman to high alumina cements with the accompanying physical differences. Within such ranges, the diviner will not merely necessarily detect an emanation for carbon, or silicon or magnesium, but for the predominating element (radiesthetically) within the compound. Indeed, in this straightforward field dowsing, there is no such thing as a compound's emanation, an alloy's or other aggregate's emanation. In ancient metals, both bronze and silver again are alloys, as only thus are they traditionally workable or durable. In having thus touched upon the value of samples, both as amplifiers and as insulators against extraneous effects, it may be fitting to mention the not-so-widely accepted theory of colour samples. And here your speaker must confess at once in fairness that he has never himself devoted much time to the investigation of this system, and so far as he personally is concerned, his results have not been as conclusive as those when direct physical samples were employed. I express it as a personal opinion therefore, that with a sample in no way agreeing in form, composition, appearance (or even colour !) with the deposit, the link is far too tenuous for reliance in such a practical class of dowsing. In any case, I have always been a little worried since a distinguished physicist warned me with some severity that strictly, colour was non-existent ! Similarly, where fully physical samples are available, I personally would never advocate the employment of mental imagery as a sample. Here again, unless one is a positive fakir, assured of his yoga efficacy at the exact moment of operation, the link is all too vulnerable for dependability.

Having touched thus, all too briefly, upon what I may call the physics of our subject, let us now pass on to a consideration of the actual apparatus most often in demand. You will readily appreciate, I am sure, that the special field problems of archæology require of us in turn special equipment to cope with them. Classed under this heading more by convenience than respect, one needs, above all, a first-class caddy-cum-comrade. Much of your success in any field work will depend upon this worthy, who must have certain qualifications. First, there should be the patient, ox-like temperament that can slither interminably through mud in your wake loaded with paraphernalia. Not least in importance too, this assistant should know enough of dowsing, and, above all of you, to be quite incapable of expressing astonishment at anything you do. In practice, husbands or wives, by virtue of their vows and other commitments, normally fulfil this miserable role ideally. The actual gear needed is simple, though difficult to restrain in one pair of arms, especially in the absurd climatic conditions that invariably obtain at excavations. As a short list one may mention the bag of wrapped samples, marking pegs and something to drive them in with, measuring tape of at least fifty feet, and, for your own sake, a camera. Also invaluable for this work, we may mention an ordinary fencing foil, sharply pointed ; not tipped. Although this sounds a wild addition, I have found it indispensable in probing meadowland down to a depth of three feet to check one's shallower emanations. But one must do this gently owing to the danger of breaking important material below. One has only to add watch, compass, sketchbook, pencils, large scale map, to say nothing of sandwiches for two, to see that our assistant has to be ox-like in more than mere temperament. It may also chance, on top of all this, that you are one of those distinguished people with bad memories. If this is so, your assistant will also carry your list of serial figures and a list of ancient units of measurement with modern equivalents.

From our brief notice of apparatus, we can move on with your permission to our actual field methodology. This does not perhaps, present any great variations from the ordinary field work we normally employ in other prospecting. Owing, however, to the shallowness, comparatively, of the deposit, with the relatively close contiguity of walls, the surface pattern of emanations can be exceedingly difficult to interpret, and, if out of reach of our epée, can take many hours of patient labour to stake out. Imagine for a moment if you will, a structure of uncertain origin some five feet below the turf. It comprises possibly, among other features, a number of small chambers adjacent to each other which seem to measure some ten feet square. It is suspected archæologically from such surface evidence as has survived, that the building is constructed of dressed limestone blocks. The site itself is bedded across a basically limestone substratum closely akin in origin and chemistry to the building you are prospecting, so that in effect, the vertical emanations rising from the structure's edges are muffled in definition by association with their underlying strata. All that the rod can here detect is the minute chemical difference existing between the quarried stone and the natural bed, a difference due solely to chemical change through the weathering of the former in the centuries before submergence. Add to this muzziness the intricate pattern of primary emanations, criss-crossed by the deposit's secondary or false (depthing) zones, and you have an absolute maze to unravel. (Incidentally, having at last made mention of a divining rod, it is as well to mention that this easily lost object, together with pendulum, is not normally entrusted to the luckless assistant. The pendulum lives quite comfortably in its small bag in one's pocket, whilst the rod, in order to keep up the bald externals of sanity (!) is in practice held quite safely in one's sleeve).

Upon arrival on site, many diviners would prefer to cross the area in a rapid cast with rod alone, without samples of any sort, the rod being held lightly so as to pick up only major lines of force. There will, as we all know, be quite a few nebulous and perhaps meaningless emanations in most self-respecting British meadows. That school of thought which believes in the amplifying effects of terrestial magnetism will here wish to select the southern or northern boundary to work from, according to whether the emanations are positive or minus. Whatever one's method or technique may be, your assistant pegs out your pattern, leaning pegs away from the walls delineated. You can thus rapidly build up a rough picture of what is " downstairs," and can tell at a glance whether the pattern thus presented is man-made or natural, or, indeed, the maddest of most mad nightmares (this last being by no means outside our experience). The curves and irregularities of geological formations are, of course, easily distinguished from the normally ordered forms of architectural structures of a past age, with their proportionate themes. But presuming that your image has in fact resolved itself into a man-made deposit, you are faced with your hardest task in arriving at any floor-plan by patiently eliminating depthing lines from main runs by their relative strengths. Successive casts across these main runs employing samples in order of probability should soon establish whether your structure be of brick, sandstone, limestone, flint or even a cement mortar filling, bearing in mind that all dressed-stone facing may have been pillaged for subsequent structures elsewhere down the ages. Having thus by sample discovered some amplifying sympathy with our deposit, it is safest to complete all wall-tracing with the sample to which you find it related. Not only will the resultant amplification reduce our error constant, but it will effectively cancel out extraneous emanations ; a most welcome aid when dealing with the crumbling and ill-defined sort of alignments typical of most ruins. With regard to isolated pocket emanations (as distinct from main lines), the pendulum comes into its own. Provided you can arrange shelter from wind and rain, the pendulum has a superior definition and an accuracy impossible in the rod. This technique is always indicated when approaching, for example, a metal object whose presumed frailty will demand an inch-by-inch clearance.

It may chance that all this can happen to you in a free-lance capacity, and that you are your own archæologist with only an owner's permission to investigate. (You should take warning in this event, for an owner's permit is of little avail against the scorn and machinations of organised archæological science, as represented by the powerful county and municipal societies, apart from the university faculties, the Office of Works, Historical Monuments Commission and a host of other vigilants. All these good and highly trained souls are properly anxious to be in on matters affecting them, especially the museums, and by enlisting public interest through the press, can effectively disturb the peace for your site and its hapless owner). But should you be, as I have said, nominally your own master, there exists of course a variety of interesting methods for diagnosing the actual type of ruin which you have thus plotted, and this long before excavation is decided upon, for example, there is a world of difference between the surface plan of a pre-Roman earthwork (or rather the subterranean remains of one) and a Roman fortified camp. And it is worth noting here, touching upon pre-Roman works, that the tiny mounds called " Tumuli " or " Tumulus " upon large-scale Ordnance Survey maps are normally Celtic barrows (or burial mounds), whose pathetic contents have long since been dispersed by the casual plough. The early British earthwork has traditionally a circular or ovoid plan, whilst the Roman camp is classically square or rectangular, with encroachments and annexes well known to every schoolboy from his illustrated history books. Perhaps it ought to be explained at this point that although no stone or brickwork occurs in either Celtic or very early Roman work, and although the suspected area is almost invariably levelled by centuries of denudation and agriculture, the site is by no means dead to a careful diviner. The minute chemical differences induced originally by the pugging and ramming of escarpments, the nitrogenous residues from timber baulks long since rotted to oblivion, the humus of years of human drainage and the phosphorescent leachings from repeated sepulture have each their eloquent whisper for a rod in the right hands. The difference in plan too, between the encampment and the villa farmstead, is, as one would expect, apparent by common sense rather than by scholarship. Coming up the scale to mediæval remains, it is no great test of intelligence to discriminate again, between the layout of castle, church, manor house or monastery, and, whatever our architectural ignorance, we have always surface references to assist us through our admirable library service, since each district has its well-documented peculiarities (many of which were enforced by the type of stone, transportation and other facilities which were available). As to monasteries and other religious houses, each order tended to develop its own well-marked fashions in building. Thus, a Benedictine abbey is recognisable alike in Nazareth, Monte Cassino or Colchester (and for that matter, in 1200, 1536 or 1957 A.D. !).

20

As to our rich heritage of fine old churches, you may perhaps feel that since they have always been centres of veneration with very few breaks, they have been carefully tended and their position and form invariably preserved. You will find, unhappily, that this is far from the case, and that the tale of neglect and, often, outright vandalism reached its peak under our early Victorian ancestors. But one must be fair and admit that the sense of responsibility in this respect varied enormously throughout the forty-three dioceses of the Establishment, but there, neverthless, remain plenty of divining problems. For example, there are many cases of whole aisles, transepts, and, as in a famous Sussex case, naves (!) abandoned to ruin owing to lack of upkeep or population drift. It is often an interesting poser to delineate the former dimensions of the building from its footings, which are still detectable by the dowser beneath the churchyard sward. Your speaker to-day is fortunate in having had a rare grounding in such problems, since, in the 'thirties he compiled in the Victoria and Albert Museum an index of the twenty thousand-odd pre-Reformation churches of England for the Central Council for the Care of Churches ; all this under Jesse windows, Norman doorways, Saxon fonts and so on. We may conclude the ecclesiological side of our subject by quoting an example typical of such cases. At St. Osyth in Essex it was long suspected by the county antiquaries that there had been a north aisle whose limits must have considerably exceeded the extant Tudor church. It will be recalled that canonically, only felons such as witches were buried on the north (or unconsecrated) side of a church, and consequently the area in question was normally undisturbed. Careful casting across the suspect area yielded a strong pattern of the long-lost north aisle, which I then checked with the epée ; the first time the values of this weapon had occurred to me. In this case, the hidden structure was dateable by the rest of the church since the divining rod plotted, surprisingly, what is known as the Oxford corner on the end buttresses. This feature, which reached the area in the early thirteenth century, consists of one buttress running out at forty-five degrees from a corner, instead of the former two at ninety degrees respectively. It is in this sort of enquiry that the divining rod excels ; cutting down subsequent excavation costs to a minimum ; reducing to a mean the time at which an inconvenient dig has to be left open, and ideally, steering excavation with that caution needful to preserve associated material from casual damage.

It remains but to remind you all that in the spacious days where builders had room to obey canonical tradition, chancel apses and the feet of tombs and graves will be to the east. But as White of Selborne, observed, the workmen must have mostly laboured on the longest days and pointed these features at the rising sun, for there is a lot of north deflection in such official eastings.

21

Bearing in mind that it must often happen that we arrive at a fairly complete plan of some ancient buried structure, it will be of great importance to have a working idea of early measurements, for these yield a mathematical clue as to the date of the building. However casual and haphazard may have been the savage Celts of these islands in their methods of construction, the reverse is true of the civilised invaders who subsequently settled here. Indeed, since the pyramids themselves, building construction has ever disclosed a fine regard for mathematics, metrology and mechanics. Even in days boasting a plentitude of slave labour and a despotic command of materials, the mechanics of construction ever demanded architectural planning. Work had to be estimated in terms of time and materials, with adjustments for local transportation and other factors. Then, as now, quantities had to be properly costed within an over-all estimate. Thus we do in fact find that in practice the dimensions of early structures among civilised peoples were finely computed in their respective proportionate themes. And not infrequently, as in the well-timbered west, the overall extent of a structure was dominated by the average length of available beams in roof trusses. It is thus easy to visualise how in those pre-steel days the height of our British oak controlled the span calculated by Roman, Saxon and Norman alike. (In like manner, incidentally, the world's naval architects down the centuries found their designed tonnages similarly restricted in an age of wooden capital ships). And this stalwart native servitor of ours, the oak, deserves a passing salute for the ages during which it so loyally housed and floated us islanders long ere we mastered the harsh ores that superseded it. Our ancestor-builders liked to fell it some time between its 100th and 140th year. Although its extreme height could be some 100 feet, it was rare indeed for botanical reasons, for the effective length of any structural member to exceed thirty feet. Thus, if on your site you have laboriously plotted something the size of King's Cross Station with no hint of medial supports, then it is definitely one of your " off " days !

Let us now briefly examine then, the sort of measurements and their multiples, that your pegged distances are going to resolve themselves into ; supposing, that is, that you have found a genuine ancient structure. And lest you feel that we have overstated the case for measurements, we are assured by Plutarch (120 A.D.) that the local building contractors used to dub the Parthenon " The Hecatompedan," from its hundred-footed front ! Firstly, if our building be Roman, our distances are going to be computable in the *passus* and its multiples and units. This was a kind of long yard of four Roman feet that was common to both Gaul and the British Provinces. The Roman foot itself (*pes*), originally the length of a human foot, was in the west the Drusian foot, and was somewhat shorter than our modern one. The ancients seem to have experienced an amusing difficulty in deciding what ought to be the perfect foot, and their attempts ranged from the Greater Ptolemaic foot of 13.98 inches (our modern inches) down to the old Italic foot of 10.83 inches. The Drusian foot in use here was 11.65 inches, or more exactly 296 millimetres. Should your site be in mediæval Welsh strata, you will be dealing with a tiny 9-inch foot, while the Scottish Middle Ages boast one of 12.064 inches. Coming up to Saxon stratum, we meet another long yard ; literally " geard," originally a man's girth. Here again, different tribes seem at a nice variance as to what constituted the healthy warrior girth, and one hale and hearty group felt that it ought to be forty-nine (modern) inches. This they called the ell, and this solid edition of it has been preserved by tailors in England to this day. The French tailor's ell seems to have remained in the region of fifty-four inches. And I may add without comment that the Scottish tailors have contrived unnoticed down the centuries to whittle their ell down to a mysterious thirty-seven inches ! Exasperated with all this sensitivity about middles, Henry the First, a massive monarch in more senses than one, declared as law, that the ell must be his own arm's length, in other words forty-five inches. He thus invalidated the old Norman French ell, or *aune*, which the Conqueror imported at 46½ inches. Henry IV confirmed this forty-five-inch verge, or yard, in 1409, but there is evidence that the measurement increased slightly after Henry VII (1485). It was finally fixed at its present standard in 1706. I regret that the metrology of our subject has detained us so long, but we have attached no more importance to this matter than would a semester of an archæological faculty, and to the diviner, who must so often labour as a blind eye, there is ready to hand here a sure system of labelling for his emanations.

Since we live in a highly-documented state in which our University youth has expended quite a lot of its pent-up energies in organised digs, you may well think, Ladies and Gentlemen, that in so tiny an island there remain scant archæological discoveries to await your talent. But such is far from the case. For despite the highly organised state of modern archæology, we must remember that although from the point of view of the ancients Britain marked the misty limits of the world's end, it was ever rich enough to justify subjection. Periods of invasion were ever followed by wide meres of intensive colonisation and settlement, and in the turbulence of the times, ruthless counter-invasion with pillage and destruction meant the wholesale obliteration, often, of quite wealthy settlements. Thus, for example, despite the vigilance of the archæological faculty, there are on an average five coin hoards a year uncovered up and down these islands. Nor are there wanting documentary hints as to the wealth of sites and materials that yet await the spade. Manuscripts that have survived, such as the survey *Notitia Brittanorum* by the chronicler

23

Nennius, are cases in point. Nennius gave district by district (*comitates*) the number of Roman villas known in his day. There are wide deficiencies in the figures given by Nennius and the sites known to-day. There are also parochial references in Domesday to edifices which to-day have left no apparent trace. Coming up to Reformation times, there are many cases where wills have come down to us detailing gold and jewelled altar furnishings for famous shrines of which there is no mention as such in the subsequent inventory prepared for the monastery in question by Thomas Cromwell. But objects described by the testator often centuries before as of gold and gems have become, by the 1536 inventories, " sylver gylte sette with glassys." The clear inference here is that some abbots and priors saw the storm coming and had craftsmen copy their best treasures. In such times, the hiding places of the original pieces must have been known only to one or two superiors under a grave vow of silence, some of whose holders have clearly died with their secret. (In this connection, it will be recalled that the plate of Waltham Abbey was recovered within living memory).

Since the recovery of such valuables can be a decided development of archæology, it seems needful here to utter a few frank confessions as to that ancient dowser anathema, the treasure hunt. This, as we all know, has brought many a good and famous diviner to his knees. There are actually, sound technical reasons (known to several of us), as to why the treasure emanation as such is so fatefully coquettish, and these are beginning to be dimly understood. But despite that, the diviner is only human, and there is a limit to his resistance to the importunity of his public. And the more famous, the more honourable and the more disinterested he is, the more importunate is his clientèle. With no sort of claims to aspire to the foregoing illustrious category, even I can confess that a quite mediocre dowsing reputation built up over a mere quarter century of divining has been wildly squandered whenever I yielded to the treasure hunt mania. Well might the ancient mystics assert the doctrine that a buried treasure is guarded by a host of dark sentinels from the spirit world !

Now allied somewhat to archæology, and thus deserving brief mention here to-day, is that class of commission in which one is asked to locate the lost place of sepulture of certain ancient and highly venerated personalities. These range from early kings to what I here choose to describe as sundry hagiographical personalities. In the latter case one can get uncomfortably embroiled in rival theologies, and, as if the divining itself were not difficult enough, you have to be a veritable Talleyrand of diplomacy in dealing with those with whom you must liaise. My own casebook for this type of commission alone is some two years old and involves sites from Rome to Canterbury. Fortunately, authorities appreciate that a problem already perhaps many centuries old, can well wait a year or two for attention.    Before leaving our field work, it would be well to remind you of such fascinating problems as that of Camulodunum's amphitheatre.    Tacitus distinctly mentions, for example, that the city (Colchester) possessed a goodly arena, but no trace has ever been found of it so far.    On the other hand, the late-lamented Colonel H. C. Davis, of this Society, and myself did plot a promising shape not far from the city which the fortunes of soldiering prevented us pursuing.    The site is still meadowland, and might make an ideal meeting for a future Congress.

My time, Ladies and Gentlemen, is nearly at end, but before our good President throws open the session to your questions, I would like to touch upon the uses of divining in what we call surface archæology.    This is defined as archæological research not concerned with excavation as such, and is normally done in our older libraries, sometimes, or in museum laboratories, upon antiquities already recovered or even the standing fabric of extant ancient buildings.    In this connection you may be good enough to recall that my own special study in archæology has been numismatics, and that I have in the past had the privilege of exhibiting to this Society important suites of Biblical coinages from my own cabinets.    In the course of this study, which I have pursued for more than thirty years, I have classified many large private and public collections throughout the world.    And easily one of the greatest problems of such a study is that of forgery (this last a forbidden word tactfully rendered by archæologists as " copies " !).    Now no two ancient coins, even from the same die, are precisely identical, either in weight or in chemistry.    Since the pieces were handstruck for example, often by slave labour, there is inevitably a difference of compression, coin by coin.    Moreover, the alloys of the metals employed remain far from constant, and apart from all this, isolated finds of the same series but from different sites will each have developed a specific chemical patination varying according to the chemical composition of the strata from which they were recovered.    All this has made the work of the copyist, both anciently and in modern times, exceedingly difficult.    But it remains a fact, that despite most expert technologies, there exist at this moment famous museums which confess to spending a surprising amount of public money upon such copies.    And for obvious reasons, some rare pieces whose authenticity may be in doubt cannot be submitted to the erosive actions of chemical analysis, in view of the possibility of damage to a valued object.    Now those among us who have delved more fully into divining lore may recall having been introduced to the plane ray theory of radiesthesia.    This principle, which employs of course the pendulum, states that when precisely like objects are placed horizontally in juxtaposition there is detectable between them a ray of affinity.    And many operators have developed an extension of this formula wherein they prefer to align the objects along a north-south line, whilst not a few hold that a torch should be switched on down the alignment. Be that as it may, the detection of the minute differences of structure and of chemistry existing between a genuine antiquity and even its most cunning copy is in fact possible in careful plane ray work. This class of research achieved an official scientific acknowledgment when the President of the Royal Numismatic Society invited me to offer a paper on this technique. Although both bold and novel, this departure from routine numismatics was, I am glad to say, well received and indeed, was favourably (if cautiously), noticed in the Annual Presidential Address for that year. (*Proc. R.N.S.*, Vol. XX, 5th Series, No. LXXVII, 1940). In closing this survey of our potential value to surface archæology, it is interesting to notice that before the perfection of infra-red photography, at least one diviner worked regularly on hidden murals in ancient churches. The late Professor Tristram was the expert famous for church murals, and in many such ancient churches Dooms and other theological motifs of mediæval times were restored by his incomparable skill ; not the least of which were those in Westminster Abbey. These priceless monuments have invariably to be literally excavated from beneath centuries of limewash and other renderings. Working from a scaffolding with pendulum and pigment samples it became possible to plot the limits of the hidden paintings; a refinement in fact of the plane ray theory.

Since we are such severely practical people, the bibliography of archeological radiesthesis is in our langugage scant indeed. Since, so far, we have rarely concerned ourselves with this class of research, such works as we have given to posterity have had little to say upon the subject. I need hardly remind you that these works are many of them admirable, ranging from autobiographical canters of the great dowsers of the past, through the occasional translations of sound foreign books, and finally coming up to the great textbook of Maby and Franklin. This latter does not claim to be the last word upon dowsing, but this and other works await your attention in the Society's library, and it is to be hoped that more use will in future be made of that facility. Any aspiring to a peculiarly exhaustive bibliography in our craft should not omit the rare, but erudite Jesuit treatise " The Divining Rod and its Implications " by Herbert Thurston (*Month*, Nov., 1934). The author of this scholarly survey, the findings of which are overwhelmingly in favour of the veracity of dowsing phenomena, was the Roman Catholic heirarchy's official observer in this country on the Council of the Society for Psychical Research. An exhaustive writer and investigator on occult and kindred subjects, the writer's survey draws upon hundreds of ancient and modern references from foreign and classical sources in the great libraries of his order. (His study may thus be taken as reflecting

26

the official attitude of Rome towards our subject). The journal of our Society has been ever vigilant in providing down the years notes of archæological activity by members of this Society. That for March, 1940, reported the discovery by dowsing of ancient masonry beneath Kensington Palace Barracks. (This was detailed more fully in the journal for March, 1947). The March, 1946, number reproduced the photograph of a mural relief showing a Hittite mining officer almost certainly dowsing (1200 B.C.). Work on the identity of an important Nazareth Biblical site was recounted in March, 1947. In June the same year appeared the first of Underwood's interesting theses upon the relationships of underground streams with the siting of pre-historic barrows. This was continued in the December number of the same year, and again in those for March, June and September of 1948. The same indefatigable worker contributed his further findings in December that year ; finally reporting again in March, 1951. An interesting contribution on Zimbabwe appeared in March, 1952, whilst the issue for March, 1955, portrayed some South African bushman paintings reminiscent of our early Hittite dowser. And finally, for what we may call a specialist form of surface archæology we are indebted to the issue of December, 1956, for a notice on the Shroud of Turin. This, Mr. President, Ladies and Gentlemen, concludes my summary of our subject's bibliography, and brings us to the end of these remarks. If I have succeeded in interesting your good selves even a little in this fascinating branch of our craft, I am well content.

## Extract from A SCATTER OF DOWSING
*Major General J. Scott-Elliot*

*Chieveley.* Now some archaeological finds. I had been asked by my stepson to investigate by dowsing the church that stands close to his home. He wished to know which parts were the oldest. While map dowsing the church and the graveyard I found what appeared to be a track that ran into his walled garden and orchard. A map dowse of the garden and orchard seemed to show signs of archaeological periods overlapping.

There are three stages to the map dowse of an archaeological site. The first is to establish the outside edge; this gives some idea of the possible type of site and may give some pointer to period. The second stage is to establish period and date. The third is to work out the layout of the buildings within the site.

When differing periods are on top of each other it does make things complicated. However, if one can get a clearly marked edge it is not difficult to date that piece of site.

Dating by dowsing is similar to depthing for oil or water. Instead of wanting to know the depth in feet below ground one needs to go back in time to the date the site was built. This can be got at by counting back from the present; or, if preferred, first find out by question and answer if it is A.D. or B.C., then count from 1 A.D./B.C. Because it is tedious to count in single years I establish the century first, then work it down by 10s, then, if necessary, count by digits.

Going back to Chieveley, it seemed that there was an Iron Age period of about B.C. 100, a Roman period of A.D. 80 and a Saxon period of A.D. 850.

Later I went to the site and found there was nothing showing on the surface, nor was there any tradition of anything there. When I did the ground dowsing it seemed to confirm the map dowsing.

We therefore decided to prove what appeared to be a large defensive ditch in the orchard. The edges of this ditch were marked carefully by dowsing and a cut 4ft. wide and 15ft. long was put down across it at right angles (see Fig. 1). After a period of very hard work we found we had a large ditch 6ft. deep and 10ft. wide. Later we made another cut across the same ditch further to the north, where we hoped to get a ditch end and thus, possibly, an entrance. Again this cut was placed by dowsing and was found to be accurately placed. This cut we believe to be over a Roman ditch of the first century A.D. It seems to be a typical Punic ditch.

In a shallow extension of the first cut we found at 18ins. depth a very large quantity of carbonised wood. This is datable by scientific means and the date of this wood came out at A.D. 800 with a margin of error of 80 years either way. So here was confirmation of a Saxon period in the site.

A third cut, again placed by dowsing, produced another smaller defensive ditch end and a piece of road. In the infill of this cut was also found a large quantity of pottery dating from the tenth and eleventh centuries, which indicates the presence nearby of the remains of a building of that period. So far we have not proved an Iron Age period; that is to come.

*Walkerdales.* As I said, dating does work—but not always. One does make mistakes. Two summers ago I was searching for proof of a permanent Roman occupation of the Banffshire coast and thought that I had found by map dowsing a Roman signal station. This by dating appeared to be about A.D. 80, so I arranged to spend a few days excavating there. Nothing showed on the surface and nothing was known of any site near there. Unfortunately, for a variety of reasons I had to skimp the ground dowsing of the site.

28

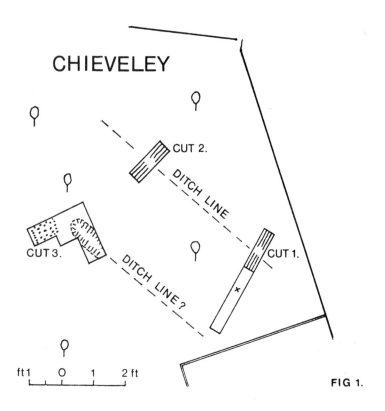

CHIEVELEY

CUT 2.

DITCH LINE

CUT 3.

DITCH LINE?

CUT 1.

ft 1    O    1    2 ft

FIG 1.

We started to excavate in two places and immediately came down on man-made structures. This was fine and we were very pleased and to this extent the dowsing had been successful. However, after a couple of days it was evident that what we had found was not Roman first century but probably medieval— about A.D. 1200.

The moral to this tale is that in all dowsing one has to be very careful. Mistakes do occur and they usually stem from bad dowsing! In this case, while the site was a new find of some interest, from the point of view of our studies it was a complete loss.

*Rookwood.* Some time ago a member of the Society told me there was a field with that name near Petersfield in which she thought there might be a site of interest, as they sometimes picked up pottery there.

So I map dowsed the site and was immediately interested, because there appeared to have been a henge monument there, also there were signs of other periods of occupation. (A henge monument is a stone circle. There are many of them in the country and they date variously about the period B.C. 2000 to B.C. 3500). Nothing showed on the surface and all that would remain of the henge might be a ditch and the holes the stones had stood in, long filled in and covered up. The soil cover was only about 6ins. and under that was sandstone.

Ground dowsing appeared to confirm the map dowsing. First we put down two small cuts 4ft. by 10ft., where I thought there was a ditch. In both cuts we did find ditches cut into the sandstone. So we were correct in thinking that there was a man-made site there. The third cut, out in the middle of the field, was designed to find one of the stone holes. The cut was 10ft. by 10ft. Here we found under the soil a man-made clay floor 8ins. thick and under that a large man-made hole in the sandstone. This had been filled with medium and small sized pieces of sandstone. When cleaned out the hole was found to be of the right size for a stone hole; one can say no more at this stage. It had been intended to carry on this year and prove a succession of three such stone holes, but this has not been possible, owing to the sale of the property.

From the dowsing point of view, here again is an example of three cuts being placed accurately, in a featureless field, on what we had expected to find.

*Daviot.* This year the owner of the House of Daviot, near Inverness, asked me if I could find any sign of the remains of a castle that was alleged to have stood somewhere near the present house. He sent me a plan of the ground concerned. This showed a narrow peninsula with sides falling steeply away to lower ground.

The map dowse came up with various things, among them what may be the southern end of a possible stone building, apparently dating from A.D. 1440. When I went there the ground dowsing seemed to confirm the dowsing of the southern end. So we put down a cut 4ft. wide over what I thought was 10ft. of the length of the wall foot. In fact, the cut was accurately placed, as we very soon came down to stone work which may be the footing of a wall some 3ft. 6ins. in width. Whether it is the footing of a castle wall has yet to be proved by further excavation.

# DOWSING FOR ROMAN ROADS

*James C. Plummer*

The above subject has been a particularly fascinating one for me, especially over the last eighteen months or thereabouts. I have become very interested in local history since I took up the subject of Environmental Studies at the school where I teach, namely, Freckleton Church of England Primary School, in the South Fylde area of Lancashire. As this part of the country has, like most of England, Wales and Southern Scotland, connections with the Roman Conquest but, unfortunately, little concrete evidence as to the extent of their activities, I have been engaging myself in attempting to find out as much as possible, by the use of dowsing rods and a pendulum.

It is an established fact that the Romans had a large military base at the village of Ribchester (Bremettonacum in Roman times). It is hard to realise that so small a place as this should have had such significance in those far-off days, but it was so and has been proved by numerous excavations, etc. over the centuries that have been performed in this pretty village in the foothills of the Pennine Range. It is known that several roads proceeded from Bremettonacum in different directions. One, a particularly fine one, according to earlier historians, left this base and proceeded into the Fylde area, taking first a south-westerly route and then running almost due west for some distance, before turning somewhat north-westerly before all traces were finally lost somewhere between Kirkham and Poulton. As just previously stated, the road (known locally as the Danes' Pad from the use that these piratical invaders made of it in later centuries on their frequent incursions into the Fylde) ran from the fort at Bremettonacum in a south-westerly direction until the town of Preston was reached (where several Roman roads have been found, running chiefly northwards). Here the road ran due west for some distance traversing the Fulwood Moor and then the Cadley Moor (these are suburbs of the modern Preston); it then traversed parts of the Fylde villages of Lea, Salwick, Clifton and Newton before reaching Kirkham, where there was a small fortlet. The route of the Danes' Pad can be seen marked on O.S. maps of the district, but its path through the latter town is not indicated. It does, however, reappear west of Kirkham, running to an elevated spot about a mile west of this town, the spot being the reservoir at the village of Westby, which helps to supply the Fylde villages with water. Beyond this point it does not appear on any modern maps, but eighteenth and nineteenth century historians spoke of the road being traceable as far north-west as the outskirts of Poulton-le-Fylde. Whether or not the road ran further north-west from here they do not say, but I personally have never accepted the theory that this large road (as indeed it has been, as readers will later see) terminated at either of these two Fylde townships. No, I could not envisage such practical people as the Romans ending a road of this one's dimensions at either of these places; I firmly believe that this road's ultimate destination lay far to the west of our present-day coastline (erosion has claimed not inconsiderable portions of the coast between present-day Blackpool and Fleetwood and land north of the latter in the Morecambe Bay area), and that this destination was a large port mentioned by the second century cartographer Ptolemy of Alexandria and referred to by him as the PORTUS SETANTIORUM (the port of the Setantii—the local Ancient British tribe of those days). Local legends support this too; at exceptionally low tides a long structure resembling an arm of a horseshoe can be seen projecting from the water; this is known by fishermen generally as " the Roman harbour."

Ptolemy mentioned this port as being 45 miles north-west of Bremettonacum and 25 miles north of the estuary of the Belisama (the River Ribble). Although Ptolemy was somewhat excessive in his measurements, these co-ordinates bring one to approximately this point where this " wall " can be found.

On the evening of September 16th, 1974, at an extremely low tide, I had, in company with a party of friends, the good fortune to visit this spot, which is north-west of that part of the coast known as Rossall Point and near the spot where the estuaries of the rivers Lune and Wyre meet. On arrival at our destination we were surprised to find not one wall, but TWO, protruding from the water and forming a shape strongly reminiscent of an ancient harbour; the shape was like a gigantic horseshoe. The structure made me wonder if this *was* indeed the remains of the port mentioned by Ptolemy, a question which has remained unsolved for centuries. I would theorise that, although erosion has taken its toll of that part of the coast, the port, if built here, would slowly sink into the waters *en masse*, on account of the solidity of its construction. The question then arose, how does one set about the task of trying to prove (a) the existence of the port here, (b) whether or not the Danes' Pad's ultimate destination was here?

After giving the matter much thought I visited a part of Newton, the village in which I live, where the O.S. maps show the path of the Danes' Pad to run; it is running approximately west-north-west at this point. The farmer whose land would have to be was traversed was approached; he proved to be most co-operative, to the point of actually taking me to the very spot where, he said, the field topsoil was no more than 1 foot (30cm) deep, before the road metal could be contacted. I thereupon thanked him and began to operate my rods, which are two simple pieces of steel wire bent at right angles three-quarters along their length, thus forming an L-shape. They are held, one in each hand, at the bend of the L, the longer portions being horizontal to the ground. They are held parallel to each other, with a gap of 27-30 cm between them, at shoulder height, and with my elbows tucked into my sides. At the point where a sought objective is reached the points of the rods swing together, cross over and form an X; sometimes the crossing is so strong that they swing right around and hit me on the chest, quite forcibly on occasions. When the objective has been passed over the rods uncross and revert to their parallel position as before.

To revert to my operations, I took up a position about 14 metres north of the spot indicated by the farmer, and commenced walking southwards towards the previously mentioned place, which incidentally was just north of a hedge. 9 metres north of the said hedge the rods swung sharply, crossed and remained so until the hedge was reached. This, I thought, seemed promising, so the next step was to walk northwards from the hedge again; at the original point of crossing the rods uncrossed as I progressed in this direction, so this appeared to bear significance also. It should be added here that all the time that I am seeking a Roman road I keep the thought " Roman road " in mind firmly and do not allow my concentration to waver at all. It is very hard work and requires tremendous concentration, and can be extremely tiring both physically and mentally, but it has been very rewarding, as I shall try to point out.

However, back to the Danes' Pad. The next step was to insert probing-rods at random points between the crossing place of the rods and the hedge. This was duly performed and in every case of insertion solid resistance was experienced between 20 and 30cms depth, thus confirming the farmer's information. As the farmer had no objection to my carrying out a " dig," the next step was to take out a trench 50-55cms wide from the hedge to the point 9 metres north of the same where the rods had crossed/uncrossed. This dig gave the following profile:—

| Topsoil | 0-25cms app. | |
| Stones | 25-37 ,, | ,, |
| Silt | 37-38 ,, | ,, |
| Grey clay | 38-48 ,, | ,, |

Yellow-brown clay (natural) 48cms—indefinite depth. The latter is the natural clay colour of this field. The grey clay varied in depth somewhat; near the hedge it was up to 15cms in depth, whereas in the middle of the road it was little more than 5cms deep. Also, near the hedge some sharp yellow sand was seen; this is certainly not natural to the area. Therefore it appeared as though here was an unnatural feature and, as it was right on the line of this great road as shown on O.S. maps, it could be concluded that here was the remains of the Danes' Pad.

The next day I visited a spot in New Hey Lane, Newton, at the place indicated on the afore-mentioned map as where the Danes' Pad ran under this lane, which is ¼ mile app. west of the farm (which is known as Moor Hall Farm). Walking in a northerly direction along this lane, I experienced a crossing of the rods at roughly the spot where I had expected them to do so, but, to my surprise, they remained crossed for a distance of between 21 and 22 metres. This seemed strange; there is something of a difference, I thought, between the measurement obtained the previous day and this, so the distance over the lane was rechecked, with the same result as before. It must be scatter area of the agger, I told myself somewhat uneasily; there was something not right and it was puzzling. My next idea was to try a pendulum. With me a pendulum produces an anti-clockwise rotation over anything connected with the male sex, and a clockwise rotation over anything connected with the female sex; when seeking an object, the pendulum will be drawn towards it with an oscillating motion. The day was calm, so wind interference with the pendulum could be ruled out. To my surprise, on using this instrument, the width of the Danes' Pad was shown as 21-22 metres, on each of three attempts. I obtained anti-clockwise rotations as I had expected, because it is almost 100 per cent sure that this road metal would have been laid down by men, whether Romans or slaves. Still, this width was a mystery, so I decided to re-visit the Moor Hall Farm the following day and proceed a stage further (or, rather, try to). These differing distances did not make sense; the Romans would not have had such different widths on one of their finest roads, as indeed this one must have been.

The next day could hardly come quickly enough. As stated previously, I do not believe in doing too much on one day. It can be very tiring, especially when one is participating in extensive spadework between dowsing operations. Still, here was a problem which must have a logical solution and I was going to try to solve it. The answer came as I was retracing my steps over the Danes' Pad in the field. Looking at the ground immediately south of the previously mentioned hedge, which is a low one, a fairly prominent ridge was discernible, running parallel to the Danes' Pad, so I tested this with the divining rods. From the hedge, for a distance of 9 metres app. going in a southerly direction, the rods crossed strongly and opened at the afore-mentioned measurement. This process was repeated three times, not in the same place, and all three results were identical, so the use of probing-rods was then resorted to. As on the other side of the hedge, solid resistance was soon encountered. The depth was 20cms app., so a trench was taken out for the whole of the 9 metres, and I was truly amazed at the resultant profile. It was completely different from the previous one and read thus:—

| | |
|---|---|
| Topsoil | 0-20cms |
| Stones | 20-32 ,, |
| Gravel and red-brown sand | 32-54½ ,, |
| Silt | 54½-56½ ,, |
| Grey clay | 56½-63 ,, |
| Yellow-brown clay (the natural) | Indefinite |

To confirm this tremendous difference in the two profiles further cuttings were made both north and south of the hedge; in every case all results north of the said hedge coincided, and all results south of the hedge coincided, to within a centimetre or two. It was clear that here were two roads running side by side; there was the remains of a ditch at the northern end (or, rather, side); this would be at least 1 metre wide; the hedge referred to so often was planted in a central ditch and there was the remains of another ditch at the southern side of this " new " road, the width again being 1 metre app. The central ditch would have been at least 1 metre, so here was the explanation as to why I had obtained repeated distances of 21-22 metres when dowsing over New Hey Lane.

On mentioning my findings to a friend, a keen amateur archaeologist, he showed me a book where a 19th century local historian had found almost a replica of my finds, at Dowbridge, Kirkham, about a mile west of the scene of my efforts; this was both very interesting and extremely gratifying, as it showed that my dowsing was correct. I should like to mention here that I do not spend time looking through books, etc. (few that there are); I like to find things out for myself by using my dowsing powers, both on the ground and over a map. The method which I employ when map dowsing is to take a pendulum, hold it over a map as large scale as can be obtained and see if any reaction occurs, concentrating intensely all the time on the object being sought. When the said object (in this case a Roman road) has been found the pendulum will oscillate along the line of the road, so the pendulum is then moved very slowly over the face of the map, to see which way the road is running. If the pendulum is moved off the track of the road it will pull towards where the road is. If, on the other hand, no road is present the pendulum produces no reaction but remains still. If the pendulum is on the course of a road and it starts either to rotate or oscillate in different directions, the spot producing such a reaction should be checked for (a) a fortlet (anticlockwise rotations) or (b) a road junction (irregular oscillations, first one way and then another). This I satisfied myself on by watching the pendulum's reaction over the map in the Kirkham area where the fort was found (and also the fort at Walton-le-Dale, near Preston). From this, I believe that this fort was not in the exact position where it is shown, but nearer the River Ribble).

However, back to my efforts to trace the Danes' Pad. Permission had to be obtained from various farmers to traverse their fields. In all cases they were most co-operative, so the course of this once fine Roman thoroughfare was followed from the original starting-point to the outskirts of Kirkham, where digging and probing had to cease, for obvious reasons. From time to time I took out a section in the fields to see if the road construction had altered at all. In some cases the road had been practically ploughed right out, but in all the digs some evidence of grey clay and scatterings of red-brown sand showed up—matter foreign to the natural terrain. The only way to find its course through Kirkham was to map dowse and operate the dowsing rods over the places indicated by the former. This was duly done (I saw several people looking somewhat askance as I worked), but the road ran through the town, not under the main street, as had been generally thought, but crossing the main road at the top of the first hill, continuing south of same through the main part of the town, and re-crossing the main road at the bottom of the second hill. It then continued on the north side of the main road, still under built-up property, until the playing fields of Kirkham Grammar School, at the western end of the township, were reached. The headmaster kindly consented to my requests to dowse the said field and dig if necessary, so dowsing by rods over the ground was performed with satisfactory results. This was followed by the insertion of probing-rods; resistance was met at 40cms app., so a section was then dug out. The last remnants of the Danes' Pad were found at 40-45cms app.—stones, some sand of a red-brown colour and grey clay overlying the natural yellowish-brown clay of the area. This grey clay appears to have formed the base of the Roman roads (or most of them) in this vicinity; it was found also in quantities in Ribchester during Roman excavations there—whether it is actually imported grey clay or a crushed limestone base which the Romans were fond of using which, due to time, has been incorporated with the natural, I would not care to opine. I gave a sample a ph. test; this read just below 7 but higher than 6.5, not very acid, which quality is generally associated with clays.

Between this point and Poulton it has not been possible, for various reasons, to traverse the land, but I have map dowsed the area, and the indications are that the road swung north-west in the region of the high point referred to earlier; from there it progressed through the villages of Great Plumpton, Weeton and on to Poulton, where, on an 1844 O.S. map, the road followed a straight boundary edge for 2½ kilometres app. It then passed through the grounds of Poulton-le-Fylde College of Education, where a dig by my daughter and myself found it again; in the

36

grounds of the said college a diversion had occurred. One road branched off to the right to meet the banks of the River Wyre at Stanah (a significant name with Roman connections), where the ground is high; the other road ran through the village of Thornton, on through Fleetwood, out to sea, and finished near the King Scar off Rossall Point, mentioned earlier. The pendulum rotated furiously in an anti-clockwise direction here; this more than anything else allows me to believe that this WAS the site of Portus Setantiorum, despite all scepticism, snide remarks, etc. that I have heard. Thinking the name of this port, I held the pendulum here and it went mad! It almost came out of my hand.

On the suggested track of the Danes' Pad through Fleetwood the pendulum was swinging near a road named Wensley Avenue, amongst many others. Later in the year I was informed that in 1967 a Roman coin bearing the head of Augustus Caesar was found in a garden in this avenue by a man digging. Could this be mere coincidence or is there something more significant in it? Personally I am inclined to take the latter view, taking into account my findings.

The road in Poulton College has been examined; here the remnants of the road were found—its width was 13½ metres app. Some red-brown sand was noticed; again this is foreign to the area and small pieces of red and yellow sandstone were apparent. The red-brown sand is reminiscent of the composition of the Kirkham Hills, which are morainic in character, and I would opine that it had been brought along the road from the latter town as the road was made.

Now let me describe my efforts to trace this Roman road eastwards from the original place of my excavations, etc., namely Moor Hall Farm, Newton. By dowsing over the ground and occasional tests with the probes, it was an easy matter to trace its course in this direction for about 200 metres, and then complications started in earnest. Instead of the rods remaining crossed for 21-22 metres, this distance was gradually widening until 25-26 metres was the overall distance, and the rods were tending to uncross for 2 or 3 metres in the middle of this distance. At this point in the field the side of the agger (the road) can be seen in an ancient cutting in the field, and there is a hollow just east of the cutting. Here was a problem. Map dowsing was out of the question, because I had no really large scale map of this area, so the alternative was ground-dowsing, probing and digging. Therefore I continued walking across the area of the Danes' Pad, gradually progressing further east as I did so; the distance soon widened to 30 metres. At this point a distinct uncrossing of the rods was observed for a metre or two. Carrying on further east, it soon became apparent that there could be not one, but two roads, one branching from the other and going in a slightly more northerly direction. The best thing to do, it seemed, was to follow the Danes' Pad and see where it ran, and follow the other later (thank goodness these were pasture fields), so this idea was resorted to. This brought me in a straight line to the south-west corner of Lund churchyard. Obviously investigations could not be carried out on consecrated land, so I picked up the road on the other side of the churchyard and traced it as far as Station Road, Salwick, where investigations on the ground had to cease. East of this road is the British Nuclear Fuels Ltd., so here was a full-stop to ground-dowsing.

It should be added here that, to check on my dowsing, periodic random digs were made along the indicated track of the sought road, and almost the same results each time were produced, namely, top and subsoil for up to about 50cms, then grey clay, sand of a red colour, and stones for 12 to 18cms below this; under this was the natural clay. At no one place was a good specimen found, but this is probably due to disturbance at some time in the past; the presence of a Roman agger would not be desirable in the days when the Fylde was a great corn-growing area. The local grave-digger told me that, when taking out a grave in the south-west corner of the churchyard, for the first two or three feet it was all red sand, stones and shingle; this was evidence enough for me. The surface of the road can be seen on the church path between the lych gate and a point halfway between this and the church -door; large stones are present all over the surface on a direct line with my dowsing. As said before, ground dowsing had to stop at B.N.F.L. but I map dowsed the area on an 1892 O.S. map and found that the road was making for Fulwood, north of Preston. I then went to the eastern side of B.N.F.L. and picked up the track of the road again, going through more pastures. The owner would not grant permission to dig. He said it was not necessary, for, a few years ago, he had been draining this field and had come across, about 2ft. down, a layer of stones about 6 or 8 inches thick on top of some strange grey-coloured clay; below this was the natural. This is south of the line on O.S. maps; I have checked on the latter and found there is a road there, too.

The course of the other track branching from the Danes' Pad has been traced to Station Road, Salwick, and there I have stopped; map dowsing on this has not yet been attempted. I can say that, by using previously-described methods, I have found:—

(1) A junction of roads one field west of Lund church, going in various directions, with some intercrossing of these roads.

(2) At least five roads branching off the Danes' Pad near the one described previously. One appeared to be making towards Preston Docks and Walton-le-Dale. Only a few weeks ago a foreman engaged on work inside the docks just mentioned said that

they had " come across a road about 8ft. down running ' that way ' (towards Walton), the top of which was made of squared sets, and it would be 20ft. or so wide."

(3) A road running west through Newton to the Dow brook on the Kirkham-Freckleton boundary, crossing this, going two fields further west, then angling at 135° and making for the latter village. Tradition says that a road ran between Lund church and its environs and Naze Point, Freckleton, but 19th century historians refuted this. Now, thanks to the efforts of my dowsings (and of two others) it looks as though this road may have been fact and not fiction. At the Naze the Romans were supposed to have had a castle/fort/port, long since destroyed (again refuted), but recently a structure has appeared, due to erosion, of a long straight wall. It has since been interfered with by backwash from ships and by vandals, but my dowsing suggests that it was Roman in origin.

(4) A building site, possibly a small Roman temple, in the field next to, and west of, Lund church. A dig here revealed quantities of flat sandstone from about 25cms, with violent subsoil disturbance at some time. Other stones were found, among them some worked red sandstone, a large erratic by the side of a post-hole, and rotten wood in the latter. Wood in the final stages of decomposition was found in the soil below 55cms, suggesting horizontal planking.

I should ike to say that I received much co-operation from local farmers and am continuing to do so. My grateful thanks should also be expressed to the following people:—

My father, though an octogenarian, is remarkably sprightly and has given a lot of help with both dowsing and digging.

My daughter Maureen Anne, who has given dowsing assistance on several occasions.

My nine-year-old son John Andrew, who has been very useful helping to mark out the tracks of the Danes' Pad and other roads by insertion of canes, etc.—all voluntary work.

My eldest son Stephen, for the publicity which he has given to my efforts.

My twelve-year-old former pupil Karen Threlfall, from Freckleton, whom I have trained to dowse successfully, and very proficient she is, too. She has given up many Saturday mornings and several evenings to help me in my efforts.

It should be stated that I have had these people dowsing at different times from each other and all have achieved the same results. The suggested temple corner-post was very positive with all three of us. It seems possible that a more complete picture of Roman activity in the Fylde may emerge as a result of these efforts.

# THE RELIGION OF THE STONE AGE

*Captain F. L. M. Boothby*

This is an appeal to dowsers for assistance in a matter which I feel sure will be of interest to many. Those who have the gift of water divining would often like to find a useful outlet for their energies, and to those of our number who are also interested in archæology, an investigation into the religion and customs of Neolithic man should prove attractive.

The simplest way to show what is wanted is to tell you how I myself became interested in the matter.

It had appeared to me that places such as the Badbury Rings in the New Forest, into which large quantities of men and animals used to retire in time of emergency, must have had more ample water supplies available than are evident at the present day, and having obtained some interesting results, I wished to consult the Curator of the Dorchester Museum about them. I found him engaged in excavating a tumulus. Having a rod with me, I tried it on the tumulus and found a spring ran through its centre. I followed up the clue, and have now tested tumuli of every type, including the long barrows, and find that they are all over springs. The long barrows mostly lie in a direction north-east to south-west, and the springs run the full length. Several tumuli are often sited on one spring. If any of my readers have tumuli in their neighbourhood, would they be so kind as to test them and let me know the result ?

The next step, after satisfying myself that the siting of tumuli on springs was no accident, was to carry the matter a stage further and investigate Stonehenge. There it was found that a spring runs right through the ruins, under the altar stone, slaughter stone and hele stone, and away down the avenue, where I have yet to follow it up.

Half a day has been spent at Avebury and Silbury Hill. The circles at the former place are sadly mixed up with the village, but it was possible to ascertain that they are traversed by a spring, and that a spring runs between two large stone blocks, called the Adam and Eve stones, and away down the south-easterly Avenue—the stones that originally lined this are now in course of re-erection.

As regards Silbury Hill—the enormous artificial hill which has been excavated on several occasions without result—several springs cross beneath it. It would appear that the whole lay-out of these ancient monuments is based on subterranean water, but until the whole has been tested it is impossible to be certain about this.

As indicated in Chapter I. of *The Modern Dowser*, there is a religious significance attached to the use of the dowsing rod in certain parts of the world to-day, and possibly dowsers of old took advantage of their gift, as Moses almost certainly did, to impress the community as well as rendering it useful service. From 1800 b.c. to the coming of the Romans the religion of this country, and possibly of the greater part of the world, may have been based on water divining. That is what we want to discover. The British Museum authorities know nothing about ancient monuments being over springs, or any possible religious significance, but suggest a search through the Library—useful work which some member residing in London might care to undertake.

It is no use *one* dowser making statements about springs and monuments—antiquarians will not believe him. It must be confirmed by others. A well-known and very competent member of our Society has confirmed that springs *are* to be found beneath every tumulus he has been able to test, and beneath Stonehenge as stated here.

What is now required is several independent dowsers—working quite alone—to trace the course of springs beneath Stonehenge and Avebury as a beginning. I suggest the results be sent to the Editor of the Journal, who can compare the results. It would simplify matters if we all used the same maps. Excellent ones can be obtained from the Ordnance Survey Office, at Southampton.


# ARCHAEOLOGICAL DOWSING
*Reginald A. Smith*


Before an audience of practising dowsers it is unnecessary to insist on the existence of radiations or the possibility of perceiving them by rod and pendulum ; and any alleged discovery of a deep spring or socket of a standing-stone will be given the benefit of the doubt, not that any observer is infallible, but because a competent dowser could test the discovery independently once a clue to the locality is given. The President's invitation to lecture on the application of this method to archæology is accepted on this understanding, and a year's work is shewn in a series of lantern slides made for the occasion and now exhibited for the first time.

In the public mind one of our chief functions or duties is to unearth treasure, and a recent case will serve both as an example and a warning. A certain village in the Cotswolds has in the lady of the manor an historian who was convinced from the records that the church plate was hidden near the church in

41

the sixteenth century to avoid the attention of Henry VIII.'s Commissioners, and the time had come to retrieve it. Naturally, the deposit would not be in the churchyard, as the digging of graves might bring it to light, and it was soon located in a farm building 100 feet from the church. The outer wall of what is now a cowshed was built in the eighteenth century, and parallel to it at a distance of about two feet a low wall was built in the last century to support the mangers, which were filled by passing along the narrow gangway in which the treasure had been located. An excavation revealed disturbed earth with chips of brick, and solid rock at about five feet, but no treasure, though the reactions for gold and silver continued. That was clearly a case of *rémanence*, and the deposit cannot have escaped notice when the footings were put in for one or other of the parallel walls. Gold and silver are notoriously difficult to find by dowsing, and treasure is always liable to disappear without trace, as until recent years the law of Treasure Trove has been considered unfavourable to the finder.

But it is with sterner stuff that archæology is mainly concerned, and it is a pleasure to mention the pioneer work done by our colleagues abroad, as the germ of this idea is to be found in Louis Merle's *Radiesthésie et Préhistoire* (1933) and Charles Diot's *Les sourciers et les monuments mégalithiques* (1935). In passing, a grateful reference to the use of the word *sourciers* for dowser, with its subtle allusion to *sorcier*; and we can briefly examine the French thesis. It is held that menhirs (solitary standing stones) and some round tumuli or barrows are watermarks, indicating the presence of at least two streams converging underground. A third stream crossing the others near the junction at the same or a different level is taken as proved, and a good deal of meaning can be extracted from the stone. The smooth front is said to face the junction and to be vertical when the three stream lines intersect; but when the crossing is between the stone and this junction, the stone is tilted away from the water; if the crossing is further from the stone than the junction is, the stone is tilted towards the junction and the transverse stream. Similarly some dolmens and tumuli are located in the angle of converging streams, and water is found to flow underground between the stone rows of the Brittany avenues.

A point to be settled is whether the height of the menhir above ground corresponds to the depth of the underground water; but the connection between some prehistoric monuments and water is established, and the conclusion is that the Druids or their predecessors were expert dowsers, and selected their holy places by discovering blind springs, that is, the heads of underground watercourses. Every religion has a special use for water, and there may have been a practical purpose in marking these hidden supplies for use in time of drought or necessity, as it would be easy to dig a few feet from the smooth face of a menhir or at the centre of a stone circle.

There is a moor in South Devon that may serve as an illustration of the French theory. Farway Down, near Honiton, exceeds 800 feet above the sea, and is dotted with barrows or prehistoric burial mounds. At the cross-roads known as Putts Corner is an isolated grass patch on which is a recumbent menhir, once erect and moved a few feet to its present position within living memory. To the west is an underground junction of two streams which flow together to the north-west. One comes from the north-east to the cross-roads, and the other from the east, being joined, on the west of a barrow which has a pond on the other side, by a stream from the north and itself flowing parallel at a distance of 500 feet. Whether the barrow contains a burial or is a cenotaph is unknown, but both the mound and the prostrate menhir may have been watermarks, about 700 feet apart.

England is fortunate in its long barrows, a type that preceded the Bronze Age series and dates from neolithic times, which ended about 2,000 B.C. These are not so obviously watermarks as consecrated sites on account of underground water, and a good example at Notgrove, Glos., was recently excavated by Mrs. Clifford for H.M. Office of Works and described in *Archaeologia*, vol. 86. An unexpected feature in the middle of its long axis was a domed chamber with a burial on its floor and a blind spring exactly at the centre. The stream from it passes out of the mound and eastward to join another : together they flow past the entrance to the burial chamber at the east end of the barrow. Wayland's Smithy, in Berkshire, is on the same principle, with variations. Its northern end is obscure, but across the approximate centre of the long axis is an underground stream, which then skirts the barrow and joins another stream, which originates below the centre of the cruciform chamber : together they flow past the main entrance, as at Notgrove.

The group of megalithic remains known as the Rollright stones, on the border of Oxfordshire and Warwickshire, is also famous in Folklore, and the theories concerning the monument are legion. The Whispering Knights, regarded as a dolmen with massive capstone, is found to have a concealed spring which runs underground to the north-west and may betoken a consecrated site ; but 100 feet to the east there seems to be another blind spring with issue to the north-east, and in view of the cases just cited, it is tempting to regard these points as the centre and chamber of a long barrow, subsequently denuded by the plough.

The King's Men of Rollright consist to-day of a renovated circle, no doubt on its original circumference, but there seems to be a smaller circle round its central blind spring and two other irregular rings outside. These would constitute a quadruple ring round the sacred centre, and the outermost includes the mysterious King Stone on the other side of the road—the only survivor of eleven on that line. There are two independent stone circles in the neighbourhood, both with a blind spring at the centre, but not hitherto mapped.

A discovery outside an earthwork known as the Berth at Baschurch, Shropshire, was published in 1907 (*Proc. Soc. Antiq.* xxi., 324) and connected with the discredited Druids, who are, however, known to have been astronomers and would have had a use for the water-clock found beside the causeway leading to the double enclosure. The bronze dates from the Early Iron Age, but there is a blind spring at the centre of the earthworks and an earlier date is possible for their construction.

The next seven cases form a group of earthworks on the same general lines, though experts would see differences and probably not agree on a common date. An oval or circular rampart, sometimes double, and interrupted by two opposite entrances, can hardly be for defensive purposes, as there is a ditch parallel to, but at some distance within, the innermost rampart. As all of them have blind springs in the exact centre and were therefore probably holy places, they can be classed as temples (in the classical sense of sacred enclosures), the congregation being seated on the inner face of the rampart, and the authorities functioning in the central area isolated by the ditch. Diagrammatic plans are given in Allcroft's *Earthwork of England.*

The best known is Arbor Low, Derbyshire, which had a ring of standing stones round the inner area, but these are now all prostrate, and there are remains of tombs near the centre, no doubt of privileged personages. The Stripple Stones at Blisland, Cornwall, have an inner area nearly 200 feet across, enclosed by the ditch. The camp above Burrington Combe, Somerset, is of irregular shape, but its section conforms to type, as did the best of the Thornborough rings in the North Riding, though this has been mutilated. A site north-east of Salisbury called Figsbury has been excavated by Mrs. Cunnington and proved difficult to explain, but the inner ditch, separated by a berm from the rampart, no doubt served as a sunk fence enclosing the sanctuary. About 1770 Pennant made a sketch of a group of earthworks south of Penrith and published it in his *First Tour in Scotland*. The southernmost has disappeared, but the others remain in inferior condition. To the west is Mayburgh, an imposing circular rampart with a single entrance, and near the centre and blind spring, is one of eight standing stones, suggesting a central chamber with passage of approach. On the east, near the river, is King Arthur's Round Table, with the northern entrance imperfect, and a circular raised platform in the middle but not concentric with the area enclosed by the ditch. This would shew the celebrant to better advantage, and no trace of standing stones has been found to mar the view. Maumbury Rings, just outside Dorchester, Dorset, is clearly of this class, but instead of an inner ditch (can that have been subsequently filled in ?) has a ramp at the foot of the earthwork as if to accommodate spectators.

All that can be seen to-day of the Castlerigg circle east of Keswick is a ring of standing stones, with a small enclosure inside, attached to the circumference, and two stray stones outside near the path leading from the west. Farmers and others who remove megaliths would normally disregard the packing stones at their base, and these, if left behind, would react like the stones they supported. Dowsing suggests that the monument originally consisted of five concentric rings, with a blind spring at the centre. There was a small one within the existing circle, and the enclosure already mentioned linked these two together. Another ring followed the existing stones closely enough, but the two outer rings were less regular, and respectively included the two outlying stones near the western path, one of which has been recently moved a few feet. The maximum diameter would be 500 feet, nearly five times that of the surviving stones.

This unsuspected diameter is, however, only one-fifth of the outer ring at Stanton Harcourt, Oxon. The three Devil's Quoits are well known, but few would imagine that they all lie on the circumference of the middle circle (or oval) of three, grouped round a blind spring that sends a stream underground to the Windrush on the west. This was probably the most extensive monument in the country, measuring 807 yards against 369 yards at Avebury.

About one-third the area of Avebury is the well-known stone circle called Long Meg and her Daughters, at Little Salkeld, near Penrith. No one living has seen anything but an irregular ring of standing stones with an outlier of imposing dimensions about 70 feet to the south-west. As at Rollright, this seems to be the only survivor of an outer ring of 13 stones, but the line is interrupted on the west, no doubt owing to the proximity of another circle that has disappeared, less regular than the Daughters and about 20 feet less in maximum diameter. Both have a blind spring at the centre, and the issuing streams join to the north of the existing circle. This, however, does not solve the problem set in *Antiquity*, vol. viii., 1934, p. 328, on the strength of a drawing by Stukeley, dated 1725 and shewing a small circle on the higher ground south-west of Long Meg. The recorded diameter of this circle is 50 feet, and a circle, in

45

the proper position (400 feet from Long Meg and of the specified diameter), is found by dowsing to have a blind spring at its centre, with the stream flowing south, and an outer circle of 300 feet maximum diameter, which, as occupying more space, would be cleared away before the smaller circle within, evidently before the time of Stukeley.

Stonehenge is a familiar sight, but there is much below ground that should be borne in mind. Excavations undertaken by Colonel Hawley for the Society of Antiquaries and H.M. Office of Works have revealed a ring of sockets in the chalk that once contained upright stones round the inner base of the ramparts : they are named after Aubrey, who mentioned some still standing in 1666. Two other rings of empty sockets between the existing monument and the Aubrey holes were quite unexpected, and are known as the Y and Z series, so Stonehenge was originally a much more elaborate structure than at present. Precisely at the centre, a few feet in front of the Altar stone, is a hidden spring, from which flow three streams : two of them unite near the north-east end of the great horseshoe, and the third flows approximately south. Here, as elsewhere, the underground watercourses avoid passing under any standing stone or socket, and it seems as if those responsible for the lay-out knew and respected these effluents from the sacred source.

An avenue or approach road has always been known to extend about 770 yards to the north-east, and Colt Hoare's rather fanciful plan (*South Wilts*, 1812, opp. p. 170) shews the northern fork pointing directly across the Cursus. An air photograph shewing the continuation of the southern branch to the Avon at West Amesbury was a notable achievement, and the line is now inserted on the Ordnance map, but the northern limb remained a mystery, and there seems to be no mention of any standing stones lining the Sacred Way. Dowsing offers a solution, and not only extends the northern avenue to Durrington Walls, but locates the stones that lined both branches in opposite pairs, the intervals decreasing from about 500 feet to 300 feet as the monument is approached. Only one stone remains as a witness— the Cuckoo stone south-west of the Walls—and this finds its place in the scheme. The fork is about 3,000 feet in a straight line from the entrance to Stonehenge, and the northern terminus once had a ring of standing stones inside the earthen Walls with an underground spring and the stone-lined avenue starting from the centre. The distance to the centre of Stonehenge is just over two miles. All hitherto known about Durrington Walls is summarised in *Antiquity* for 1929, and excavation recommended as a last resource. From the terminus near the Avon to the centre of the monument by way of the southern avenue is rather more than 1½ miles, and the terminus was perhaps never complete, as dowsing reveals a blind spring in the centre of a broad oval, of which the southern half is represented by a single find.

Another feature of interest in the neighbourhood is the Cursus, generally regarded as a prehistoric race-course. It runs almost east and west about half-a-mile north of Stonehenge, and its width is 350 feet. It is traceable from the rounded end on the west for 3,000 yards to what is mapped as a long barrow right across it, but the mound has no blind spring as a long barrow should have, and is apparently a later obstruction, as the Cursus can be traced to a rounded end about 840 feet west of the Cuckoo stone, making a total of 3,730 yards.

Between the (restored) south bank of Durrington Walls and a long barrow near the Avon is a remarkable monument, also discovered from the air, and given the name of Woodhenge in contrast to its famous neighbour nearly two miles to the south-west. It has been carefully excavated and a monograph produced by Mrs. Cunnington, of Devizes. The plan shews six concentric ovals (nearly circles), and the sockets found in chalk subsoil for wooden posts are now marked by concrete stumps. In the centre a blind spring is revealed by dowsing, and from it flow two streams northward, threading their way between (not under) the closely grouped sockets. In the sacred enclosure, a few feet from the centre, was found the burial of a child.

There are several cases of earthen or stone circles arranged side by side but not quite in a straight line, and much ingenuity has been wasted in the attempt to explain their orientation. Dowsers will probably agree that the centres were fixed by the discovery of hidden springs, and therefore by geological conditions, not by astronomical calculations. The celebrated megalithic circles of Stanton Drew, Somerset, can be explained in this way. An underground stream starts in the centre of the southern ring and joins another from the centre of the large middle circle, the course then being to the north. The small northern circle also has its hidden spring, the stream flowing into the neighbouring river Chew. Other good examples are the Hurlers in Cornwall and the set of four earthen rings of the same size at Priddy on the Mendips. Here a subterranean spring sends out a stream south-eastward from the southernmost of the four. The stream from the next on the north eventually joins that from the centre of the northernmost, and the fourth has its central spring, but the stream is absorbed by a pond close to the centre.

Few of the standing stones at Avebury now survive, but are sufficient to prove the former existence of a grand circle on the top of the ditch opposite the rampart ; also two double circles almost in a north and south line and somewhat east of the centre —an unsymmetrical arrangement that requires some explanation. If the semicircle of Aldwych were completed by encroaching on the Thames in front of Somerset House, its area would correspond to that of Avebury within the ramparts, and the true centre is a little north-east of the cross-roads. By dowsing methods a very different picture is presented, and the original monument seems to have consisted of four multiple circles almost in a line, much like those noticed above at Priddy. The southern circle is always represented as double, but close round the central blind spring there is evidence of another small circle, and the underground stream passes eastwards under the rampart just south of the eastern (modern) entrance. Within living memory there was a standing stone at the centre—a most unusual position over a spring.

Near the centre of the next double circle, just north of the east-and-west road through the village, are still three stones, a large and smaller standing and the third discovered by Mr. St. George Gray, prostrate and in three pieces just below the turf. It is a curious thing that at the centre there is no underground spring, but on analogy one formerly existed and subsequently failed. The Cove is now found by dowsing to belong to an irregular square of stones, as though five rows of five stones had been spaced to form a covered area, the roof being probably of timber. A third circle within the northern rampart has been suspected, but never planned with conviction, and what is now submitted is a quadruple ring irregularly planned, with an underground spring at the true centre and stream flowing west, but surrounded by a figure with parallel sides and pointed ends. As the northern arc of this group encroaches on the ditch and rampart, it may be inferred that the stones, ditch and rampart of the great circle belong to a later period. Outside the rampart and astride the Swindon road is a fourth double circle with blind spring in the centre of the inner ring but the outer ring not concentric. The stream flows directly to the east, and the maximum diameter is 350 feet.

Superimposed on these four sacred sites was the great circle, surrounded by a stupendous ditch and exterior rampart. As noticed above, the inner slope of the earthwork was intended for spectators who were kept off the sacred enclosure by a ditch proved to be about 25 feet deep. From the exact centre, two streams issue from a subterranean spring, and flow eastwards, perhaps at different depths. Both would supply a small pond in a farmyard as well as the large pond in the fosse, where they terminate. Two inner circles belong to this later period, but the only stone of which there is any memory was the Ringstone, located by Stukeley near the southern entrance. There seem to have been twelve other stones in this ring, which has an average diameter of 900 feet. Still nearer the centre, but flattened on the eastern side, was a third ring of fifteen stones, passing through the centre of the southern ring and having an average diameter of 530 feet. Two stones were common to this and the northern ring just within the ramparts, respectively 100 feet north and 160 feet north-west of the Cove.

To the southern entrance of Avebury there was an avenue of approach from the south-east, formerly flanked by standing stones, of which several exist about midway between Avebury and the village of West Kennett. It is known as the Kennett avenue, and was considered by Stukeley to terminate in a stone circle called the Sanctuary on Overton Hill, about 1½ miles from the Avebury entrance. He lamented the destruction of this circle in 1724, but the site has been excavated by the Cunningtons (*Wilts. Arch. Mag.* xlv., 300), and no less than five concentric rings of stone and timber posts established, with a few outside bearing witness to the avenue. The form is slightly oval and the maximum diameter 130 feet. Dowsing reveals a blind spring at the centre (indicating its original sanctity) and also the complete course of the avenue, which was not quite straight. The reconstruction of its northern end is described in *Antiquity*, 1936, 418.

Whether there was ever another approach to the western entrance has long been debated, but Stukeley had little doubt of its existence in the Beckhampton direction. He was, however, a student of serpent worship, and identifying the Sanctuary on Overton Hill as the head of a serpent, he endeavoured to locate its tail at the Long Stones, about a quarter-of-a-mile north of Beckhampton. This attempt showed that all trace of the avenue (except close to Avebury) had been lost in his day, but by dowsing it can now be traced with the sites of its flanking stones for a distance of 1¾ miles to another Sanctuary, with its oval enclosure and central spring, on the downs south-west of Beckhampton. The very twists of the Kennett line are reproduced, and the great mound of Silbury is equidistant from the two avenues, evidently forming part of the great scheme. The Long Stones are found to be the remains of a double circle round a blind spring, like four other ruined circles on the same quarter-sheet of the 6in. map (Wilts. xxviii., S.W.). Such circles, like the barrows, might be expected near a religious centre, but the selection of this area for cult purposes was no doubt due to the presence of underground springs in the first instance.

Results obtained by rod and pendulum are apt to be personal, and dowsers may disagree as much as archæologists as to their accuracy and interpretation, but the constant presence of underground water at the exact centre of these earthworks and circles is a significant feature easily verifiable by others in the field. If this be allowed as intentional, the Druids or their predecessors, as the spiritual and intellectual leaders of their people, come at last into their own, and the selection of sites for consecration no longer appears arbitrary, but dictated largely by geological conditions, of which advantage was taken to advance religion and at the same time to provide an emergency water supply by means of a series of permanent and conspicuous monuments. Any new light on the ancient Britons should be welcome to students, not only in this country but abroad, wherever dowsing is becoming a subject of serious study in spite of "scientific" opposition.

# ARCHAEOLOGY AND DOWSING: Part I
### Guy Underwood

Archæology is the study of antiquity. It is a fascinating occupation. It is too fascinating, and for the last two years I have done practically nothing else than dig, survey and record, and study in stuffy libraries.

One of the mysteries, which has inspired much erudite speculation among antiquaries, is that of the location, arrangement and design of the prehistoric Stone Circles, Long Barrows and Round Barrows. They are usually referred to as " sacred sites."

As to location, there is no obvious visible factor common to all that will provide an explanation as to why they are placed where they are.

*Long Barrows.*—These are enormous oval burial mounds, sometimes over 300ft. long. They are usually on heights, but sometimes not. The date of erection of these is usually placed as between 2500 and 1900 B.C., that is to say, during the last half of the Neolithic (or late Stone Age) period.

They have the peculiarity that the larger end is, in the great majority of cases, directed towards the East. This orientation may vary from a few degrees E. of N. in one case to a few degrees E. of S. in another. The ancient peoples were quite capable of orienting these mounds precisely—what then was the consideration so paramount as to lead them to vary their sacred orientation ? Why also, if they were of so great importance as appears, are they not all sited in the most prominent positions ?

*Stone Circles.*—The dates of the Stone Circles are about the same as the long barrows, but some may have been built somewhat later, and there is evidence that others, for example Stonehenge, have been altered and partially re-designed at later dates. The sites of circles also vary in their heights, most are high but some, for instance Stanton Barrow, Avebury and Long Meg, are in low-lying situations.

50

Most Stone Circles have outlying stones, clearly related in some way to the circle, the significance of which is a complete mystery. At Stonehenge there are two " Station Stones," lying N.W. and S.E. of the circle. Somewhat similar stones are found at Woodhenge, Stanton Drew, and many others.

*Round Barrows.*—These are almost all of the Bronze Age, 1900 B.C. to 500 B.C. They are found at all heights and are often found in groups forming straggling lines. Why ?

Attempts have been made to explain these peculiarities on astronomical grounds, or by alignments, but nothing appears to have carried conviction except in the minds of the propounders of the theories.

It is clear that, having regard to the enormous labour of erecting these great monuments they must have been regarded as of the highest importance. It follows that their locations are unlikely to have been haphazard or arbitrary, and that some cogent reason must have decided it. This reason must have formed an important integral part in the prehistoric religion. If that reason can be discovered, it would provide a far-reaching addition to our knowledge of prehistory. The object of this article is to submit facts which appear to have some bearing upon this.

So far as I am aware, the first archæologist to call attention to the apparent association of underground streams with pre-historic sites was M. Louis Merle of Capdenac, Aveyron, France.

His book on the subject, *Radiesthésie et Préhistoire*, published privately in 1933, is a pattern for protagonists, short and simple, and gives nearly forty scale drawings of sites, showing clearly the courses which are taken by the streams which he alleges are associated with the remains. Anyone able to dowse should be able to verify the statements without difficulty.

1. *Burial Mounds.*—He states that prehistoric burial mounds in France are always located in the *fork* caused by the junction or crossing of two or more underground streams, and are usually enclosed by three or more such streams.

2. *Menhirs.*—These are solitary standing stones of large size, sometimes called monoliths. He says (*a*) That these are placed in the fork of two underground streams, which are also crossed at or near their intersection by another stream.

(*b*) That if the menhirs have one smooth side then this side will face the junction, and

(*c*) That if the three streams cross at the same point, then the stone will be vertical, but if one crosses between the junction of the others and the stone, then the stone will lean away from the junction, and if one crosses beyond the junction, then the stone will lean towards the junction.

51

3. *Alignments.*—He states that the celebrated stone align-ments of Carnac, Morbihan, are set between roughly parallel streams, and that any branching or connection with another stream is indicated by a stone of larger size than the others. He gives a plan of Carnac, and also of linear mounds at Reilhac, Lot, where he states that the mounds follow the lines of a complex of streams.

As to menhirs, it seems likely that many such supposed monoliths may be solitary remnants of former stone circles or of burial chambers.

If menhirs were, in fact, boundary marks, as is generally supposed, they would be more likely to be placed at the exact intersection of the streams rather than at some distance away. The leaning of the stones and the alleged smooth sides could be due to age or other causes.

In a later book, *Les Sourciers et les Monuments Mégalithiques* by Chas. Diot, published privately, 1935, the author confirms M. Merle's observations. He becomes mystical and adds little that appears to be useful.

In 1935 a similar discovery was made, apparently quite independently, by Captain F. L. M. Boothby, C.B.E., R.N., a member of the British Society of Dowsers, who contributed a short article on the subject to the *Journal* (*B.S.D.J.*, II, 115).

Captain Boothby was interested in the water supplies of the great prehistoric camps existing in many parts of the country. Some of these would need 5,000 men or more to defend them, and with the men would be their families and animals. Such a congregation would be likely to need about 10,000 gallons of water a day to keep them alive.

Few of these camps show any surface indications of wells, and the usual explanation given is that they relied upon dew-ponds. To anyone with knowledge of the possible supplies from dew-ponds, such an explanation is absurd. Others allege that sieges, contrary to historical records such as the siege of Troy, etc., were unknown in those times,* and that warfare consisted in a short sharp attack, after which, if it failed, the attackers presumably called it a day, and went off home !

There is no reason to suppose that our ancestors had less common sense than we have, and it must have been obvious that, having got their enemies onto the top of a high hill on which there were no adequate water supplies, all they had to do was to wait until the defenders were thirsty enough to surrender !

---

* *Earthwork of England,* by A. Hadrian Allcroft, 1908 ;  page 210.

It is unlikely, also, that the defenders would have put themselves into such a position. They must therefore have made wells, and all that is necessary to prove it is to dig until they are found. Some wells have been found—for example at Maiden Castle—and Aubrey states that a spring existed within the Badbury Rings. The difficulty in finding these wells is largely due to the ancient method of storing grain. This was in pits, belling out as they got deeper, dug into the earth. In some camps hundreds of these pits have been found, and the reason suggested for this large number is that fungi made it impossible to use them more than once or twice, as otherwise the grain would spoil. The surface indication of such filled up pits cannot be distinguished from those of filled up wells.

In *Water Divining* by Theodore Besterman, p. 93, the author quotes a letter to him from Captain Boothby, dated March, 1937, in which he says : " The most interesting work I have done in England was in connection with tumuli and ancient monuments. It was found that all tumuli tested have been erected over springs. Stonehenge and Woodhenge are also on an elaborate system of springs. It seems probable that this has some religious significance. Plans of the system of springs on part of Salisbury Plain are with Colonel Bell and the Curator of Salisbury Museum, if you require them."

It is a pity that Captain Boothby, in common with some other dowsers, refers to underground streams as " springs." A spring is the place where an underground stream emerges. This is, however, a minor point, and his contribution to the subject is great. (1) His statement that barrows are located over underground streams anticipates and agrees with that of later observers. (2) He states that in the case of " long barrows " these streams usually run their full length—in other words, that they are aligned upon them. And (3) That " several barrows are often sited on one spring," which explains the straggling lines of round barrows so often found on Salisbury Plain and elsewhere.

All those who have made a study of antiquity are familiar with the name of Reginald Smith. He was a famous archæologist, author of many papers on the subject, and the leading authority on prehistoric implements. His reputation was world-wide and extended wherever prehistory was studied. He is still quoted as an authority. For many years he was Keeper of the British and Mediæval antiquities at the British Museum, and was Director of the Society of Antiquaries.

He was a somewhat dour and reserved Lancastrian—he did not suffer fools gladly—but could be most kind and helpful to a student who, before asking questions, had taken the trouble to learn something about the subject (a rare circumstance !). He retired from the Museum in 1938, and died on the 18th January, 1940. He was not a man likely to put forward any important proposition, on his own special subject of prehistory, unless certain of the grounds for his conclusions.

Towards the end of his career he began to take less interest in his formerly beloved flints, partly owing to the continual empty contradictions which are a depressing feature of modern archæological research, and partly, no doubt, owing to the fact that this part of archæology appears to be at stalemate—all possible useful information likely to be squeezed from such objects having already been extracted.

He began, therefore, to turn his attention to a wider aspect of prehistory, and to explore phenomena which he had noticed on his many visits to prehistoric sites in this country. His observations of these phenomena were the subject of a lecture given by him to the Society on February 15th, 1939, which was published in *B.S.D.J.*, III, 348.

M. Merle's observations as to French prehistoric mounds differ from those of Mr. Reginald Smith and Captain Boothby in this country. Both of the latter state that sacred sites here are situated directly over streams, and not in the fork of converging streams. If M. Merle's statements are verified, it would appear that the prehistoric religion in France differed in this respect from that in this country. All of them agree, however, that such sites in both countries are located at places where peculiar complexes of underground streams exist.

A few years ago I made investigations into some of the alleged phenomena of dowsing, with a view to separating them into flocks of reliable sheep and unveracious goats ! Included in these tests were the observations of Boothby and Smith. I visited a number of ancient sites for this purpose and found that their statements were confirmed in all cases. Sketch plans of some of the sites visited are given in the illustration.

With regard to the sites illustrated.

## LONG BARROWS

*Lugbury, Littleton*, near Chippenham, Wilts.—This is a characteristic long barrow, about 180ft. x 75ft. It has a clear example of a " blind spring " in its East end, over which the primary burial chamber has been erected. It is also interesting for being aligned E - W over parallel streams, running its full length, a feature found in several other barrows. Most of the transverse streams, of which there are many, have been omitted for clearness. As to the four secondary burial chambers on the south side— the most easterly one is crossed by four streams. The other three are practically free from streams, although surrounded by them. See Merle's observations as to barrows in Brittany. Secondary chambers are unlikely to be earlier than the primary,

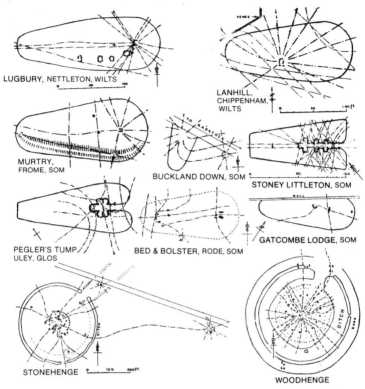

LUGBURY, NETTLETON, WILTS

LANHILL, CHIPPENHAM, WILTS

MURTRY, FROME, SOM

BUCKLAND DOWN, SOM

STONEY LITTLETON, SOM

PEGLER'S TUMP, ULEY, GLOS

BED & BOLSTER, RODE, SOM

GATCOMBE LODGE, SOM

STONEHENGE

WOODHENGE

The courses of underground streams are shown by broken lines.
Stones are indicated in black, except Stonehenge, where standing stones are in black and others in outline.

and are usually later. Many of the Bronze Age invaders, who supplanted the neolithic people in this country, came from Brittany.

Only the primary chamber is now visible, and the remains consist of three stones, standing about 7ft. above ground. One of them is 12ft. long. A measured survey of the site has been made, showing all streams.

*Lanhill Barrow*, near Chippenham, Wilts.—This is an unusual long barrow, as the primary chamber is in the middle of the mound and not at the east end, as is more usual. The blind spring is clearly seen. Most of the transverse streams are shown, and the parallelism, irregular spacing and difference in angle suggests that they are rock fissures caused by seismic waves coming from at least two directions. Rough survey by pacing only.

55

*Murtry*, near Frome.—This site appears in the Ordnance map as " stones," but has the appearance of being a much-damaged long barrow. The blind spring is clear. It has two standing stones over the centre of the spring. One of these is 9ft. above ground. Surveyed by pacing.

*Buckland*, near Frome.—Blind spring is clear. Rough survey by pacing.

*Stoney Littleton*, near Wellow, Somerset.—This is the finest example of a chambered passage-grave long barrow in this country. The parallel lengthwise streams are clear, and there appear to be several blind springs with centres between these streams. The barrow is aligned upon the parallel streams, which lie N.E. - S.W. Carefully surveyed by measurement. Some unimportant streams omitted for clearness. Scale plan available, showing all streams.

*Hetty Pegler's Tump*, Uley, Gloucester.—A very fine example of chambered barrow. Superficial survey only. A blind spring appears to be located at the centre of the cluster of burial chambers.

*Bed and Bolster*, Rode, Somerset.—This site is almost destroyed, but some stones remain. It is given because of the two length-wise streams. Appears in the Ordnance map as " Burial ground." Rough survey only.

*Gatcombe Lodge*.—Long barrow. Stream traverses two burial chambers. Not completely surveyed.

*Winterbourne Stoke*.—Long barrow. Not illustrated. This barrow is about 300ft. long and about 15ft. high, built of chalk. It is about 1½ miles S.W. of Stonehenge. It is aligned on two parallel streams running S.W. - N.E., and has a blind spring with about 10 radiating streams under its N.E. end, which is the larger. It is very similar to Lugbury.

*Jug's Grave*, Farleigh.—Not illustrated. This is a newly discovered barrow, of the end of the Stone Age or beginning of the Bronze Age. A central primary burial chamber, or " cist " was found containing skeletons. In the body of the mount, outside the cist, there were a number of secondary burials in the manner peculiar to the late stone age (neolithic period). The primary cist was enclosed within streams, but not crossed by any. The other burials were all at points where streams intersected.

This barrow is surrounded by a number of enclosures, amounting to about 15 acres, which are themselves bounded by long mounds, usually called " Celtic field divisions." These were possibly originally stone walls.

These enclosures are remarkable, as they do not appear ever to have been ploughed, but to have been left derelict since the site was finally deserted and allowed to return to forest. In these enclosures the courses of the streams after leaving the barrows are marked by large stones set at intervals in, and level with, the ground, and particularly at any intersections. In some cases these stones extend for a distance of over 100 yards. Surveys are being made, and I hope to publish the results shortly.

The other barrows on the site exhibit similar peculiarities, and are now being excavated and surveyed. All are on blind springs.

### CIRCLES

*Woodhenge.*—This is an ancient temple, and originally consisted of a number of concentric circles of wooden posts. It is generally supposed to be older than Stonehenge. It was discovered from the air in 1925 by Squadron Leader Insall, V.C. It is one of the most important of modern discoveries, and an example of what may result when new methods are applied to old subjects. It has been fully excavated, and concrete stumps mark the position of the old post-holes. The 60 stumps of the outer ring make it easy to survey and to check the streams shown.

There are two blind springs, one under the centre and the other under the grave near the centre; in the grave the bones of a child were found. There are 20 radiating streams, and about the same number of transverse streams. The latter are not shown in the drawing, for reasons of clearness. A survey has been made.

*Stonehenge.*—The complication of the streams here is extreme and cannot be shown in a small illustration. Only the principal streams (observed on a casual visit some years ago) are shown, therefore. It has now been more fully surveyed, but by pacing only, and a scale plan prepared. There are about 30 radiating streams and a large number of transverse fissures.

There are two blind springs, one under the altar stone, and another a few feet in front of it, in the centre of the circles.

It will be noticed that a stream passes under the two " station stones," C and D, and under the centre of the circle, and leads on to the barrow about 150 years east of the monument. This barrow is located on crossing streams, as is usual with round barrows. The Hele Stone H is also on crossing streams, as shown. One stream, not shown, appears to connect the Hele stone with stone D and another to run from it to the barrow within the circle.

The immense number of fissures here make it difficult to follow and record the exact course of particular streams, especially the transverse streams. The radiating streams are more easy to follow.

### ROUND BARROWS

I have so far examined only one group—that at Winterbourne Stoke, on Salisbury Plain, near Stonehenge. Here there are about 20 barrows. The centres of all of those examined were at points where several water-bearing fissures cross, and all barrows appeared to be connected to each other by streams. About 10 of them are in an almost straight line, from the long barrow, in a N.E. direction, and all these appear to be on one stream and at points where other streams cross it. I was told, locally, that another dowser had surveyed this and other nearby groups, presumably Captain Boothby.

## BOUNDARY STONES AND MISCELLANEOUS

It is often impossible to say from visual evidence only whether any large single standing stone (called *Menhirs* or monoliths) is or is not a solitary remnant of some larger structure. It is generally accepted, however, that where they do exist they are boundary marks, similar to the stone pillars known as *hermae* in Greece. All ancient stone boundary marks that I have found have been related to underground streams.

*The " Three Shires Stones,"* on the Foss Way, five miles north of Bath, were erected, or re-erected, about 100 years ago on an older site. They are on the crossing point of three streams, one of which crosses the road at right angles and the others diagonally south of it.

*The Long Stone*, Minchinhampton, Gloucester.—This stone is said to run round the field at midnight. It is also said that if children are passed through a hole that is in it they will be cured of rickets ! It is on a blind spring, and is probably the remains of a burial chamber.

*Bathford Hill*, Bath.—There is a footpath along the top edge of the Avon valley, running from the " Dry Arch " about one mile beyond Bathford and five from Bath. It leads past a tower called Brown's Folly, and then bends east towards Box. It runs for about a mile. On the east side of this path there is an old stone wall, which marks the boundary between Wiltshire and Somerset. In this wall are set, at irregular intervals, large stones, half buried in the earth. Other large stones are in the open West of the wall. There are about 20 of these stones, many of which are shown on the 6in. Ordnance map. Each marks an underground stream.

This is a lovely walk, 500ft. above the river and overlooking three great valleys and the city of Bath. It is well worth a visit, apart from its dowsing interest.

Similar walls exist, a few miles away, at Warleigh and Freshford, also on the boundary. I hope to deal more fully with boundary marks in a future article.

## ARCHAEOLOGICAL DOWSING

It will be noticed that at Woodhenge and Stonehenge many more streams were found than were reported by Boothby and

Smith. I use, however, rods more suitable for indicating the weaker reactions than they used, and would recommend others to use sensitive rods for this purpose so as to get all the streams. With such rods the centres of stream bands can be located within a few inches. A good rod can be made from two knitting needles and a piece of wire, and is described elsewhere in this issue. If a twig is used I would recommend one of thin whalebone.

There are over 30,000 barrows in this country (L. V. Grinsell, *The Ancient Burial-Mounds of England*, p. 1), so that there is ample scope for those wishing to test these things. There are also numerous stone circles, dolmens, &c., at all of which the characteristics described should be present.

Generally speaking, all rock formations in this country, especially the limestone and the chalk, are much fissured by seismic disturbances. The fissures are roughly parallel with each other and at right angles to the direction of the siesmic waves causing them. If they are waterbearing, the courses of these fissures can be traced easily by dowsing. They can be distinguished from what the dowser calls " parallels " by the fact that they are not at equal distances apart. In surveying some of the sites mentioned, these parallel reactions were very noticeable, and seem to indicate that all the streams are in rock fissures.

It is significant that the great majority, if not all, of " sacred sites " in this country are located where a rock subsoil, usually limestone and chalk, exists near the surface. It is difficult to imagine how a blind spring could exist, and persist, in any other than a rock formation.

Substantial underground streams are seldom near the surface. In the limestone district, with which I am most familiar, the depth to water is usually over 100ft. There are, therefore, no surface indications.

The primary facts of dowsing are not universally accepted and are sometimes denied strenuously by people who have made no proper investigation into them. The task of anyone wishing to put forward any proposition involving dowsing is therefore made doubly difficult by some dowsers, who make assertions of apparently miraculous phenomena, of which they may have heard or read, but which they have not tested properly. When put to the test, they fail. They thus disprove their own cases, bring dowsing into disrepute, and create a body of opponents among the very people whose opinions are most respected, and who could be the most valuable in establishing the facts. A good example is the following incident :—

When I first became convinced of the truth of Reginald Smith's theory, I thought it wise to look round for an expert archæologist who was also an expert physicist. Such a man should be capable of reliable judgment on both subjects. At last I found such an individual, and wrote a tactful letter. He replied in a most friendly way, but said that he could not accept the alleged facts of dowsing. His reasons were that some years previously a well-known dowser visited his excavations, and, among other things, claimed that by the use of coloured rods he could indicate the presence of buried metal objects. The dowser said that violet-coloured rods would indicate bronze. He proceeds : " To put his claim to the test, I excavated in his presence several large and deep holes . . . where he claimed bronze existed. No evidence was forthcoming, and he finally agreed that his claims could not be substantiated." A valuable recruit was thus lost to dowsing, and a weighty opponent created.


# ARCHAEOLOGY AND DOWSING: Part II
## *Guy Underwood*

The test of the connection of dowsing with prehistoric structures can be made with little difficulty. The best site is a round barrow of the Bronze Age, of which large numbers exist in the country. A few barrows of the Roman and Saxon periods have been found, mostly in East Anglia, which will be unlikely to show the characteristics described, but the great majority of round barrows are of the Early and Middle Bronze Ages (1900-1000 B.C.),* and on all these there should be found a number of intersecting streams, usually called a " blind spring," at the centre of the barrow.

If this is confirmed by other independent observers, then the proposition that dowsing formed an integral part of the prehistoric religions should be established in the minds of all reasonable people.

Such a proposition, however, is of great and revolutionary importance in archæology. It will be fought tooth and nail by many, and wide acceptance does not necessarily follow proof for a considerable time. The most ingenious arguments will be produced by the captious to throw doubt upon it. It is an unjust world !

Interesting examples of blind springs and of the obsession of the ancients with underground water are given in Fig. 1.

The site is of the Bronze Age, and contains three barrows.

* The dates of the prehistoric periods are approximations. As there was no history there can be no known dates. Those given in these articles are conventions fixed by a committee, and many people disagree with them to the extent of hundreds of years. They have the advantage that they enable the comparative length and order of the periods to be appreciated more clearly. They also give a pleasing appearance of precision to our observations.

It is enclosed on three sides by long mounds, usually called Celtic field walls, but in this case possibly of earlier date than the arrival of the Celts, which began about 750 B.C. The boundary on the S.E. consists of a sloping bank known as a lynchet. Numerous oak trees grow on the site. The subsoil is limestone, and the upper soil, below the humus, is brash. The whole enclosure covers about two acres, of which about half is illustrated. The other half does not contain so many streams.

The central barrow, " A," has 16 streams radiating from its blind spring ; " B " has 14 and " C " 11.

It is of outstanding interest that this enclosure, like those around Jug's Grave previously referred to, appears to have been undisturbed by agriculture since it was abandoned. It seems unlikely that this abandonment occurred later than about A.D. 60, when the last representatives of the prehistoric religions in this country were suppressed by the Romans.

The ground surrounding the barrows contains about 250 stones, all recumbent, except one which is standing. These stones appear to mark the courses, and particularly the intersections, of underground streams, most of which come from the barrows. Only about 25 stones are not in positions related to stream courses, and it is possible that some of these may have been disturbed by the felling and removal of trees which has, no doubt taken place periodically. The existence of these stones suggests that similar water marking stones may have existed on other sacred sites elsewhere but have been removed. One of the first things done by a cultivator is to remove large stones. Practically all such sites known have been under cultivation at some time or another.

A line of large stones N.W. of Barrow " A " has much the appearance of outcrop. I doubt this, but as yet none of the stones around the barrows have been disturbed.

Barrow " A " contained a circle of standing stones (called a peristalith) arranged round the central burial chamber or " cist." Seven out of eight of these stones marked places where fissures radiated from the centre, and there were four stones on the outside edge of the barrow marking places where four other fissures very close together emerged. The courses of eleven out of the sixteen streams were therefore marked and it is difficult to suppose that this was accidental. Other standing stones may have existed formerly but may have been disturbed by roots or other causes.

The dowsing reactions found on prehistoric sacred sites are seldom strong. One reason may be the dissipation of the available water into a web of small fissures Few of them would provide substantial water supplies—a fact that has probably saved many ancient monuments from destruction.

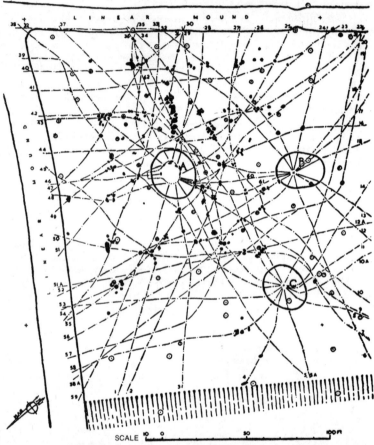

FARLEIGH WICK, WILTS

SACRED ENCLOSURE NO. 6

'THREE BARROWS'

VISIBLE STONES
OAK TREES
STUMPS OF TREES
EXCAVATIONS
INFLUENCE LINES

FIG. 1.—Prehistoric site containing barrows all sited on "blind springs" and showing stones which appear to mark the courses of underground streams.

The tracing of streams with a sensitive rod can be done at a good pace. The stream, when found, is followed by criss-crossing it diagonally, and the rod will give a good and clear nod each time the stream is crossed. The dowser should try to proceed in a straight line. He will soon notice if the stream bends, by the failure of the rod to indicate. The direction of the bend is easily found, and the dowser then continues as before, but on the new line. A marker should be put down periodically on streams that do not run straight, and on complicated sites it is an advantage to mark the course of each stream with thin string, so that it will not be confused with other streams, can be verified, and its course recorded later. Fissures often cross each other at narrow angles, but if marked by strings their courses can be checked with ease. See later as to surveying.

There is often misunderstanding as to underground " streams " in the minds of the uninitiated. Some of them seem to visualise babbling brooks running a few feet below the surface ! They find this proposition difficult to accept, and are liable to doubt all other statements made by the dowser. As streams in stone formations usually run in fissures, it may avoid misunderstanding if they are referred to as fissures until some more esoteric word can be found. This appears to be one of the few known instances of insufficient jargon in any art, cult or profession.

The facts are that underground water, usually at considerable depth and pressure, forces itself through beds of gravel or sand, or narrow fissures in the rock, trying to find an outlet where its pressure can be relieved. Some idea of the depth and pressure of some streams can be obtained from the hot springs at Bath. Here the temperature shows that the water must come from at least 3,600ft. below the surface, and that the pressure, at its full depth, must be well over half a ton to the square inch. Such a pressure is considerably in excess of that in any normal high pressure steam boiler. It is only in places where the rock is of a kind particularly soluble in the acids carried by the water from the surface, as, for example, in the Mendips, that free-flowing streams are found running through caves. Such streams can be seen at Cheddar and Wookey Hole.

It seems a pity that so much emphasis has been placed on water in connection with dowsing. The fact that it is possible to find water supplies by dowsing is an isolated and, possibly, minor phenomenon of a far more important physical fact—the existence of a geophysical force so far not identified. The inclusion of the word water in the name water-divining seems to dilute the importance of the subject as much as that liquid detracts from the effectiveness of other, and by some considered more precious, fluids.

Most of my readers will be aware that there are two kinds of dowsing influence—positive and negative. The narrow line of influence above the stream is positive, and the broad bands of influence on each side are negative.

It is not so generally known that there are two kinds of dowser. The normal dowser is more sensitive to the positive, while the so-called " ultra-sensitive," " village " or " natural " dowser feels the negative more strongly. In country districts the village dowsers are almost all of the latter type. They number only about one in several thousand of the local populations, although some others have the peculiarity without realising it. It is probable that it is the rareness of this particular kind of dowsing sensitiveness which has led to the erroneous idea that only a few specially gifted people can dowse, a statement which the village dowser makes frequently. The special sensitivity of this kind of dowser appears to be due to a peculiarity of their nerve centres. I have made some experiments which seem to confirm this, and see also Dr. J. A. S. Elmslie, *B.S.D.J.*, I, 3, p. 47 and II, 10, p. 106.

When a number of streams are close together, as on a sacred site, the wide negative influence bands overlap, become confused and cannot be followed. The narrow positive bands, however, remain clear, and can be distinguished at a distance of a foot from each other. A negative dowser, therefore, cannot locate the streams of such sites. I have tested this several times with competent village dowsers.

I have also tested similar sites with dowsers of the positive type. They had no difficulty in finding and following the streams illustrated in Fig. 1. In two cases, independently of each other, they pointed out that I had omitted stream No. 51a from my plan, although unknown previously to them.

It follows, therefore, that the ancient priests must have been positive dowsers, that is to say, normal people who had learned or been taught to dowse in a special way, rather than natural dowsers of the negative type.

It is known that water had a religious significance to the prehistoric peoples and, as Reginald Smith pointed out, every religion has a use for it. He also suggested, however, that menhirs and other isolated standing stones were watermarks for use in case of public emergency.

Although prehistoric sacred sites were associated with underground water, I doubt whether the water was of any utilitarian importance to the ancient dowsers. They must, however, have realised the connection of water with dowsing, as underground streams can often be traced to where they break out as springs.

I have only found evidence in one place of any distinction appearing to be made between strong and weak streams. This is at Freshford, Wilts., where the largest stones mark the strongest streams.

It seems unlikely that the ancient peoples had any need for artificial water supplies. Wells become a necessity only with large populations. In the later Iron Age there was a great population in this country, and Caesar, who paid us visits in 55 and 54 B.C., tells us that the population was " innumerable." We have no reason, however, to suppose that this country was as

64

thickly populated nearly 2,000 years earlier, although we do not know for certain.

We do know, however, that the people of those early times could not sink wells in the limestone or harder rocks, as they did not possess the metal tools essential for the purpose. It follows, therefore, that the association of water with sacred sites and with menhirs and similar standing stones, had no relation to water supply, although probably considerable relation to water sanctity.

SURVEYS

Sometimes the dowser may wish to make a record of what he has found—in other words, to survey it. The equipment he will need is as follows :—

A surveyor's 100ft. tape measure.

A number of markers. I use bamboo canes 2ft. long for markers, and 3ft. and 4ft. long for special marks.

Thin string and something to wind it on.

A compass.

Sectional paper and a note book.

A canvas bag to carry the markers, similar to a small golf bag, which can be slung over the shoulder, is useful.

Small stone circles, such as Woodhenge, near Amesbury, and The Sanctuary, near Avebury, are easy, as the positions of all former stones are marked by concrete posts.

Round barrows are also easy. After finding the blind spring, a marker should be inserted in the centre and two more North and South of it and at equal distances. These three will make your base line. Two more are set at the same distance from the centre at right angles to the base line, so as to make a square, and string is laid round the four outer markers to show the line. Do not cut the string, as knots are a nuisance.

Draw the square to scale on sectional paper, and also the rough outline of the barrow, marking the North or any permanent feature on to which the base line has been aligned.

The radiating streams should first be marked by laying down markers near the centre, and then all positive reactions on the outside of the square should be marked by inserting markers.

Starting from the nearest marker to where you have tied the string, trace that positive reaction. If it leads to the centre, wind the string round the centre marker and trace the nearest stream from the centre to the outside, and so on. Mark any transverse streams. When completed, lay your tape measure along one side and mark the streams on your plan, and so on until all sides are completed. This is the best test of dowsing and of dowsing skill that I know of, as two good dowsers should produce identical plans independently of each other.

A long barrow is more difficult. A base line should be made

65

along its long axis, with large markers every 50ft. Similar lines should be made on each side, at equal distances from it and with similar markers. This will produce a rectangular enclosure called a grid. Then proceed as with a round barrow. You may need 200 markers and several pounds of string and several days to do it.

You cannot use string if there are cattle in the field, as they will eat it. It is disconcerting to both parties to have to pull many yards of string or tape measure from their cuds, and it spoils the tape measure.

Every small object that you are likely to use and lose (rod, pencil, indiarubber, &c.) should be tied on to yourself with string. I have lost many such things in the grass. It is a good idea to tie something bright red (plastic tape, procurable at Woolworths, is good) to every object, in case you drop it.

The most difficult sites are those with large open spaces and few permanent marks.

The subject is vast, and there are many questions which one individual alone cannot investigate. For example : Had the direction of flow of the water in the streams any significance ? Long barrows are usually aligned upon two parallel fissures, and are usually oriented with their larger end towards the East. I have never been able to distinguish the direction of flow of a stream, but some dowsers claim to be able to do so. If they can do so, it seems probable that the ancients could do it also. It would be interesting to know whether the direction of flow of the water is always the same in relation to the larger end.

As to long barrows aligned on streams, but not oriented it would also be interesting to know the direction of flow and the ultimate courses of the streams. A good example of the latter type of barrow is Belas Knapp, near Cheltenham, which I have not yet been able to survey. It is the only known example in the Cotswolds of a long barrow which is not oriented. It is one of the most perfect long barrows in Gloucestershire.

" Supposition " is really another name for theory. Theories stimulate enquiries and can be very useful. They are also very enjoyable. Mine are therefore : First, that it was good magic, and, secondly, that its primary practical use was for fixing boundaries.

Magic is the exhibition to the uninitiated of the effects of controlled physical forces. We have much evidence that magic formed a large part in the prehistoric religions, and also that the priests made a study of natural philosophy, or what we now call physics. I have heard it propounded that the methods of Joshua in dealing with persons with whose opinions he did not agree suggest that he had a knowledge of explosives ! The peculiar mystery of dowsing must have provided an added attraction—even now we do not know the cause.

66

As to boundaries, here dowsing would be particularly useful. Boundaries so fixed are unalterable. If the marking stone was moved, the priest could identify the spot from which it came. He would gain much kudos by doing so, as both the criminal and the injured party would know the true facts. Boundaries were of particular importance to the ancients. The functions of the deities Thoth, Hermes and Mercury included the fixing and maintenance of boundaries. There are also indications suggesting its use in the laying out of processional ways or " Avenues."

Although Reginald Smith refers to certain complexes of underground streams as " blind springs," I am inclined to think that some of them must be merely multiple intersecting fissures. The name. " blind spring," however, is convenient. They were not the only geological features sacred to the ancient peoples. Other and rarer geological peculiarities exist and appear to have been of greater sanctity.

Blind springs were associated mainly with barrow burials, but are often found also in the centre of stone circles. There does not appear to be a blind spring in the centre of the large circle at Stanton Drew, near Bristol, although there is one in each of the smaller circles there. I doubt whether a blind spring was regarded as sufficient by itself to justify the erection of a Circle. I am inclined to think that, associated with all stone circles, there will be found certain features which I propose to describe in my next article.

Burial in barrows is generally taken to have commenced in this country at about 2500 B.C. and to have largely ceased with the end of the middle Bronze Age at about 1000 B.C. All the barrows of that period appear to have been on blind springs.

Blind springs are in the nature of geological freaks, or remarkable coincidences, as it is obvious that towards the end of the 1,500 years of barrow burial they must have become increasingly hard to find, and, in the end, practically exhausted. It would be interesting to know whether this was any part of the cause for the change of burial customs in the late Bronze Age. During that period, burials were mostly in urns set close together in cemeteries called Urn Fields. I have so far only tested one case. There, although associated with streams, there was no indication of a blind spring. One of the streams, however, appeared to link the urn field to a nearby barrow.

The proof of a theory is in its application, and I have recently been applying this one to our principal prehistoric monuments— Avebury, Stonehenge, Stanton Drew, &c. About all these there are many things which are not understood and upon which archæologists have argued for generations. For example, much ink has been expended on trying to find an explanation for the two " Station Stones " at Stonehenge. Another question is— Why is the Hele Stone exactly where it is, and not nearer or farther away from the monument, as it could be without destroying its supposed function as a dial stone ? In my last article,. it was shown that dowsing supplies reasons for these.

As to Avebury—What is the reason why the main Avenue takes the course it does, and what was its course where not known ? How many avenues were there, and what were their courses ? What is the meaning of the apparently inexplicable line of stones found recently in the South Circle ? Why is the Great Circle not circular ? There are many other such questions, but above all is the paramount and overwhelming question— Why are these great monuments located where they are ? If the answer to the latter question can be provided, it would affect archæology vitally wherever the remote past is studied.

Dowsing appears to throw light upon most of these questions.

Few experiences are more fascinating than to travel in an undiscovered country, or in one that is new to us. Most people have been enthralled by those stories of H. G. Wells, Dean Swift and Samuel Butler which depend for their attraction upon the comparison of experiences in our own country with those in other places where values are different and where things are done for what seem to us to be no good reason.

For the last six months I have been doing the same, but have gone backward 4,000 years into a community where every important religious action, and therefore presumably many others, appears to have been governed, or at least affected, by geological conditions.


# ARCHAEOLOGY AND DOWSING: Part III
*Guy Underwood*

My work on this subject has been temporarily interrupted. I propose, therefore, in this article to give only a few further instances illustrating that water-divining was part of the prehistoric religions, and to limit myself to facts such as can be verified without the need of elaborate plans.

So far as dowsing, apart from archæology, is concerned, I suppose that the most important thing I have discovered is that certain influence lines perceptible by the dowser are not continuous but are sometimes found to be broken, apparently by the effect of other, and presumably stronger, lines crossing them. Where they are broken the influence lines turn back upon themselves, taking a semi-circular or spiral course very similar in form to the letter " J " or sometimes with a double spiral not unlike an anchor.

I also found completely circular influence lines on several sites :

that is to say lines which when followed brought the dowser back to precisely the same spot from which he started. As a general rule they were roughly circular but not precisely so. See The Sanctuary later.

Both of these discoveries are of great interest to archæology, as they solve problems that have baffled archæologists. These are—the reason for the ditches and mounds usually encircling prehistoric sacred sites, and for the mysterious breaks or " causeways " found in them.

CIRCULAR DITCHES AND MOUNDS

Many prehistoric stone and other circles have a ditch and mound surrounding them. Stonehenge, Avebury and Woodhenge have these. The Budbury Circle at Bradford-on-Avon had a mound with a ditch on each side. These ditches and mounds are not defensive in object as the ditch, or the larger ditch, if more than one, is usually inside the mound and therefore no hindrance to an enemy. The explanation usually given is that the mounds were stands for spectators and that the inner ditches where they existed were to separate the public from the consecrated centre of the circle while ceremonies were taking place. The ditch at Stonehenge is, however, outside the mound.

These ditches are seldom truly circular, and that at Avebury is about 50ft. longer in one direction across the circle than it is in the other direction, and is very irregular in its outline. It is a fallacy to suppose that our ancestors of 4,000 years ago, and particularly their priests, were completely untutored savages incapable of erecting structures with precision. It is known that they possessed knowledge of some of the sciences, and the priests, at least, are likely to have inherited some of the culture of Egypt and Mesopotamia, the supposed cradles of their religion, and with which they were likely, therefore, to have had occasional communications.

An example of their capability is in the circle of great stones at Stonehenge, which is the most prominent feature of that monument. This circle is truly circular on the inside, and is composed of great stones about 20ft. long, weighing up to 30 tons, set vertically, and (as they are seldom more than two or three feet deep in the ground) balanced on their ends so skilfully that they have stood erect for several thousand years. These facts show that the ancients could make a true circle, that they possessed sufficient mechanical skill to erect these great stones precisely to it (a feat which would be quite creditable nowadays) and that they must have had a knowledge of how to find the centres of gravity of these vast irregularly surfaced stones. This would entail accurate measuring instruments, a knowledge of mathematics, and considerable skill in handling these stones. It follows, therefore, that where these circular ditches and mounds are not truly circular they were made so deliberately. That being so, there must have been a reason for this irregularity. The question therefore arises—What was this reason ?

What I have found is that these ditches and mounds follow the courses of roughly circular influence lines which were usually found in sets of three. The bottoms of the ditches follow these lines, with one line in the centre, and the edges, where the banks meet the flat bottom (quite clear in places at Avebury), following the outer lines. If these lines splayed out further apart from each other, as sometimes was the case, the ditch would get wider and *vice versa*. If there was any clear irregularity in the approximate parallelism of any one of these lines with the others there would always be some irregularity in the bottom of any undisturbed ditch to indicate that something unusual was to be found at that spot. This could be a raising of the bottom of the ditch on one side to show that the line veered to that side, or in some cases, by a deepening or shallowing of the whole ditch. The same conditions applied on the tops of the circular mounds and fully explained the otherwise incomprehensible irregularity of vertical outline and wavering courses. The great ditch and mound at Avebury show all this very clearly, particularly as the bottom of the ditch retains in some places approximately its original shape.

I do not, of course, suggest for a moment that these circular influence lines indicate the existence of circular water-bearing fissures. I think that there is little doubt that they are harmonic reproductions of primary influences some distance away, similar in nature to the " H " bands described in my article in the *B.S.D.J.* 46, which are lines of influence found between the stream band and the inner parallel and between each pair of parallels. Their circular form here appears to be due to the combination of a number of these influences, from within and outside the circle. If this is so, they have, therefore, some resemblance to what the electricians call lines of equipotential or to the interference lines found in wave motion.

There is another peculiarity of prehistoric circular ditches which has greatly interested archaeologists. This is that they are not continuous but have " causeways," that is to say, that they appear to have been filled up in places. Excavations show that they never were continuous, as the natural and undisturbed soil or rock which can be found at these places show that they are intentional. These causeways are not set at regular intervals, and there are often more of them than appear to be necessary for ingress and egress from the circle. Their existence is usually regarded as evidence that the ditch was constructed in the late Stone Age. The reason for them is one of the problems which archæology has never been able to solve.

Dowsing throws considerable light on these causeways.

What I found was that they mark places in the circular influence lines where such lines have themselves been interrupted by other influences. Where they are interrupted they are turned back upon themselves in " J " spirals or whorls as before described. At such places you will find, therefore, six of these whorls in the case of a ditch and mound, or nine if there are two ditches. It is therefore possible for the archæologist dealing with a ditch and mound which has been destroyed to locate and peg out not only the courses originally taken by the ditch and mound, but also to locate the places where these causeways will be likely to be found. This, in my experience, places in his hands an instrument of incalculable value, as very similar phenomena exist in association with all parts of early prehistoric religious structures.

The great circle at Avebury has five of these causeways, through four of which roads now pass. The other is a little north of the east entrance to the circle. Stonehenge has twelve of them, some not yet excavated.

The double sets of three influence lines, with interruptions in them, described above, are not restricted to circular structures. They also occur in the mounds and ditches of the rectangular earthwork 1½ miles long, known as The Cursus, near Stonehenge. Their presence there seems to indicate that that structure has causeways, and is therefore contemporary with Stonehenge.

## STONE AVENUES

Among the many other interesting things I have found is that the stone and other " avenues " associated with our prehistoric monuments are all aligned upon systems of parallel fissures in a similar manner to that described by Louis Merle as existing at the great avenue at Carnac, in Britanny. Carnac was originally about eight miles long, and consisted of eleven rows of great stones. It is now partly destroyed.

*Stonehenge.*—The avenue here runs from the Hele Stone, taking a semi-circular course in a westerly direction, ultimately reaching the Avon at West Amesbury, 1½ miles away. Part of its course is marked with low banks on each side, and each of these runs between two fairly closely set fissures. There are eight parallel fissures in the avenue where it reaches the great circle, and over a dozen where it crosses the main road at West Amesbury.

The influence lines of the avenue fissures are interrupted and terminate in spirals south of the Hele Stone and before reaching the circular ditch. They cannot be traced within the circle, although it seems probable that the fissures do traverse it. Seven of these influence lines reappear on the other side of the circle outside the ditch, and continue across the by-road and then for a short distance before spreading out, and terminating.

The most northerly of these influence lines terminates with a spiral in a nearby barrow, presumably erected to mark the spot.

The next two terminate in spirals not marked by barrows. The next one takes a southerly direction and crosses the main road by the cross roads, and the three southerly lines remain parallel, ultimately encircling and terminating in a large barrow in the south-east corner of this field.

*Avebury. West Kennet Avenue.*—Most people know the avenue of great stones which leads from Avebury to 1½ miles through West Kennett and then turns west up to The Sanctuary stone circle described later. This avenue is aligned on a system of parallel fissures, and each line of stones is set between two fissures. There are eight fissures where it joins the great circle, about twelve in the middle and six where it enters the Sanctuary.

North of West Kennett these fissures divide, and some branch off in a S.E. direction passing West Kennett Manor and crossing the river about 100 yards east of the bridge. Two stones mark the place where it crosses. These fissures finish at the Swallowhead Springs about half-a-mile away. It is possible, therefore, that another stone avenue formerly existed here. A large stone, partially buried, can be seen at the corner of the lane and the main road, which appears to have marked its course.

*Avebury. Beckhampton Avenue.*—About 200 years ago the great antiquary, Dr. Stukely, prepared a plan showing the supposed course of another avenue formerly leading from Avebury through Beckhampton, and finishing in a valley below a small hill on which is a coppice known as Fox Covert.

Dowsing indicates that this avenue did not follow this course or pass through Beckhampton, but suggests that an avenue did emerge from the west side of the great circle, passed across the present churchyard, and divided into three parts at Avebury Trusloe Manor, ultimately re-uniting at the S.W. corner of the "Long Stones Field" near Beckhampton. From there it continued along a lane of remarkable width and across the Calne main road, and on for half a mile, finishing ultimately in two spirals in Fox Covert, close to a line of barrows. There were formerly eight in number ; all are on blind springs.

As to the Avebury avenues of West Kennett and Beckhampton, these, with the great circle, make a curious pattern not unlike the " serpent and disc " symbol found in prehistoric sites in many parts of the world, and particularly in Egyptian temples. For this and other reasons he became obsessed with the idea that Avebury was a temple devoted to serpent worship, a theory which may quite possibly be correct, although the reasons on which it was based may not bear critical examination. He believed that the Sanctuary (see later) represented the head of the supposed serpent.

Dowsing does not support the suggestion that the circle and avenues were artificially designed to represent the serpent and sun-disc, but rather that both were located for geological reasons,

72

that is to say, on parallel fissures or geophysical influence lines. Serpent worship forms part of the oldest religions throughout the world, and the reason for it is not known. It is always associated with water and fertility. The serpent is identical with the dragon and other ancient monsters. Sun worship is a later religion which was never able to oust the old religion of the serpent, and was therefore combined with it, hence the sun-disc and serpent symbol referred to before.

DOUBLE SPIRALS

Another interesting thing is that when certain influence lines are interrupted by more than one external influence they take on shapes similar to a C or an S. These are fairly common wherever an elaborate complex of underground streams exists, and particularly, therefore, on sacred sites. So far as I remember, I first found them at Avebury. They are sometimes quite small, and to trace these the dowser must see that his rod re-acts every time he crosses the influence line, and he must cross it at every step he takes.

Sometimes, however, the C and S spirals are large and show a number of coils at one end, one inside the other like a clock spring. The largest number of such coils I have found is twelve. Although the S spirals are usually between 10 and 50 feet in length, sometimes they are of great size, and one at Avebury is 1,000ft. long and links the south and central circles together.

Frequently these C and S spirals will be found in groups or clusters crossing each other, and where this occurs in an avenue a stone is usually located on the intersection point, and the more complicated the cluster the larger usually is the stone. The two lines of stones in the West Kennett avenue are about 60ft. apart. It is a peculiar fact that the centres of such clusters as I found in the avenue were almost exclusively located within the parallel influence lines between which the great stones are set.

These clusters of spirals have the appearance of blind springs, the radii of which have been interrupted and have taken a spiral form at their ends. This gives them, when drawn, some similarity to the tentacles of an octopus.

There are several blind springs of this type at Avebury—one in the centre of the yard in front of the Red Lion, another on the grass triangle where two roads meet; another in the yard of adjoining stables. There is a small one of eight radii enclosed by the two stones of " The Cove," which is supposed to be the centre of the central circle, and there is one near the west of Silbury Hill marked by a stone. The most important one of all is in the centre of the south circle. This was at one time marked by an enormous stone, now destroyed. I have found

73

only one elsewhere, and that is near Oswald's Tump, Marshfield, Gloucestershire.

The figure is an illustration of some of the geophysical conditions existing on the prehistoric site known as The Sanctuary, Overton Hill, near Avebury. It is five miles from Marlborough, by the side of the road from that town to Devizes.

The site was excavated by Mr. B. H. Cunnington about twenty

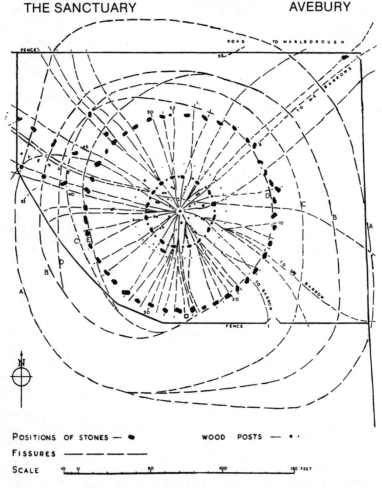

THE SANCTUARY          AVEBURY

POSITIONS OF STONES — ●          WOOD POSTS — ● ·
FISSURES ——— — —— —
SCALE

years ago, and the position of the stones and posts which formerly stood there are marked by cement blocks. This makes my plan easy to check. The circles originally consisted of wooden posts, but at a later date, probably between 2,500 and 1,700 B.C., some of them were replaced by stones. These stones were cleared away by a farmer about 150 years ago.

One important feature is omitted from my plan. This consists of two almost perfectly circular influence lines in the centre of the circle. The larger of these two has a diameter of approximately 50ft. and is marked by the central circle of stones. Within this circle there is another smaller concentric circular influence line 20ft. in diameter, the course of which is marked by eight postholes.

## TRACK LINES

*Guy Underwood*

Since my last article I have found something that seems to me to be of such interest and importance that I hasten to put it on record in the hope that other dowsers will investigate it and publish their results.

It must have occurred to most people to wonder why our country lanes, and the hedges, walls and ditches which make our field divisions, wind and twist in a completely incomprehensible manner. Many explanations have been suggested. As to the lanes the most popular one is that they were originally cattle tracks ; another is that the twists are due to gradients or to obstructions now cleared away, or that they take their courses on account of the peculiar shape of the fields.

If, however, these suggestions are considered carefully, particularly on the moors or downland, it will be observed that the facts show a regrettable lack of co-operation in that they seldom fit the theories. For example, there are no fields on the moors, and it is far more likely that tracks preceded the fields. On the chalk downlands I have seen no signs and little likelihood of any such obstructions ever having existed. Cattle, when not grazing, are usually driven by man, and take the line he wishes them to take. Neither do the paths always take the easiest gradients. It seems obvious that there must be some other and important reason which caused all the old country lanes of prehistoric origin throughout the country to take these devious courses, instead of going direct from point to point as one would have supposed would have been natural and far less trouble, and as, in fact, the roads made by the Romans did.

What I have found is that all these tracks, lanes, roads and field divisions are aligned on dowsing influence lines which I call "track lines." These are very similar to, but clearly distinguishable from, those of water ; and the reason for the winding courses

of the lanes and hedges is that they are controlled entirely by
the courses of these influence lines. These lines very frequently
run parallel in pairs, usually at a distance apart of about 15ft.,
but often at distances of about 10 to 60 feet. The lanes are
located between these lines. The existence of the lines can be
verified by dowsing in almost any field gate, or where there are
no hedges or walls, on each side of the tracks.

Many of our main roads follow these prehistoric tracks, and it
is easy for the dowser to locate places where the road has been
widened or its course altered.

Fig. 1 shows a road junction which illustrates this clearly.

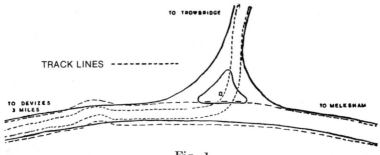

Fig. 1

These lines are not found on Roman roads or on those of later
construction.

Field divisions are usually located on single lines, and the
existence of these can also be verified in gateways.

I very much doubt whether the track lines have much, or any,
relation to water. Most dowsers are aware that all positive
influences associated with underground water—that is to say,
the stream-band, the parallels and the sub-parallels (or H1 and
H2 bands) are composed of three parallel influence lines, of which
the centre one is always considerably stronger than the outside
influences (or M bands). Track lines differ from water reactions
in that they are always composed of three sets of three parallel
influence lines, of which the centre line, that is to say, the fifth
from either side, gives the strongest reaction. See Fig. 2.

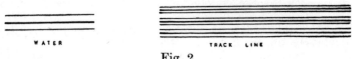

Fig. 2

They are also weaker than any ordinary stream-band, and, in
my experience, can only be distinguished in their nine separate

76

parts by the use of a sensitive rod, and by care and patience.*
They can, however, be *located* with a " twig," but if that is used,
the dowser is likely to get only one reaction as he crosses them.
The twig is slow in action and needs a fairly strong influence to
make it work. It has been pointed out in previous articles that
the dowsing influence is cumulative, and what appears to happen
is that the little influences of each line build up as they are
crossed until there is sufficient to move the rod. A " sensitive"
rod, however, held properly, will give a clear kick forwards as
each of the nine influence lines is crossed. The dowser may
not get all of them the first time he crosses the line, but if he re-
crosses it he will probably get them, and will have little difficulty
in selecting the fifth (centre) line, which is the one I usually follow
in open country. Often, however, on roads, he will be com-
pelled to follow an outside line, as the hedges or other road
boundaries were usually set upon the centre line. An interesting
fact which I have often noticed is that once the dowser has picked
up an influence line, however weak, and however many others
there may be, he has little difficulty in following it, even if it
is crossed by, or practically follows the same line as, others.

Track lines vary considerably in their strength—occasionally as
strong as stream-bands, but usually weaker, and sometimes so
weak that it is possible to cross them many times without noticing
them.

I have seldom noticed any parallels associated with these track
lines. They also appear to run continuously and to form a network all over the country. I have found them in all parts of
the west country whenever I have looked for them, and I have
also found them in the London parks.

In Regents Park the northern part of the road which leads
from York Gate into the Inner Circle is aligned, in the way I
have described, upon a pair of parallel track lines. These splay
out east and west at the circle and appear to continue round it.
See Fig. 3. Traced in the other direction, these lines cross the
large lake at an island by the bridge and continue roughly parallel
with the lake until a junction with other track lines is marked
by a great mound (M3) in the park just north of Hanover Terrace.

There is a mound (M1) by the ornamental water in what was
the Botanical Gardens, which appears to be a barrow of the
Bronze Age. It marks the terminal points of three great spirals
which encircle it. The little island (M2) in the ornamental water
appears to be another, and marks a spiral. I more than half
suspect that the Inner Circle follows the line of a prehistoric
sacred Circle.

* To get faint dowsing influences such as those of track lines, the rod must
  be held in a critical state of equilibrium, with the hands steady, and the
  dowser should move slowly. With the " link " rod it is best to hold it by the
  wire (and not by the sliding handle) and with a good pressure on the rod.

This proposition is not so fantastic as it may sound—the site of Regents Park has always been open country. It was designed and laid out by John Nash in about 1812, and he, no doubt, took advantage of, and was influenced by, the topographical features which he found there.

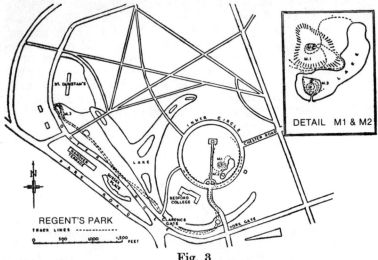

Fig. 3

I was only able to spend a few hours on the survey, and hope that other dowsers will check my statements. Regents Park is conveniently situated for Londoners to test whether the track lines I have described have or have not a factual existence, which is the first and most important question. Possibly others will complete my survey.

It seems to me that the most likely explanation of track lines is that they are associated with fissures in the rock subsoils which underlie the whole country, all of which is fissured in various directions owing to seismic disturbance. Such fissures would naturally be continuous and connect with and be crossed by others. Occasionally track lines are found taking zig-zag courses for a few hundred yards in a manner strongly suggesting that they are following the lines of fissures. I can see no explanation of the tendency of track lines to run in pairs. Where they do so, however, I have usually found a very faint influence line centrally between them. The usual width of single track lines is four to ten feet.

These lines are easily mistaken for water influences, and I and other dowsers have often done so. I have found numerous wells that have been put into them. Although I have made a study of dowsing for some years, I have only during the last few months realised their existence and the distinction between them and the water influences. The fact that wells have been sunk into them successfully is not in my opinion unassailable evidence that these influence lines are due to water, and there is, as I have pointed out, some evidence that they are not—for example, the frequent absence of parallels. On the other hand, many fissures are waterbearing, and such must have parallels.

In my last article I referred to circluar influence lines upon which the ancients located the ditches and mounds which surround some of their stone circles, and pointed out that these lines were interrupted in some places and that it was at such places that causeways across the ditches are to be found. These lines

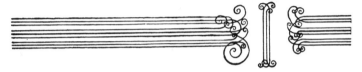

Fig. 4. Track line with typical interruptions.

are of the same type as the track lines which I have described, and the latter also exhibit the peculiarity of these interruptions. Where these occur all the nine lines are broken and turn back in spirals. See Fig. 4.

The interruption is usually crossed by spirals.

The track lines which I have described are by no means rare, and many of them do not appear to have been made use of. They can be found in open country where there is no visible sign of tracks or field divisions. Often, however, their courses are marked by linear mounds, ditches or large stones, particularly at bends and at places where they cross each other. The stones built into walls at Freshford, Farleigh Wick and Bathford Hill, described in my first article on this subject, were of this kind.

Dowsing suggests that the large, dry cavities resembling ponds, and often called dew-ponds, are really marks where track lines cross, and that they are not intended so much to provide water supplies as to guide the traveller. Archæologists usually call these depressions " pond barrows."

The fact that track lines are so often found in connection with roadways, ditches and linear mounds naturally suggests the enquiry whether they may not actually be due to some electrical phenomenon consequent upon disturbance of the earth's surface by man. This, however, is not so. As stated, I have often traced them across chalk downs where the turf is only a few inches thick and where, therefore, any disturbance at any time would be permanently visible.

The trouble taken by the ancient people to mark the courses of these lines, particularly in the neighbourhood of their sacred sites, is extraordinary. The great ditch and mound at Avebury are a good example. The town in which I live is built on the steep sides of a great valley sloping down to the river. The north side of this valley here takes the form of a series of terraces lined with old cottages which are quite famous. I have always supposed that these terraces were a natural feature probably formed when some earthquake split the hills and caused the valley. The edge of every one of these five terraces is, however, marked by track lines, and I now think it probable that the valley side was cut away into terraces by the ancients merely to mark the courses of these lines. All these lines ultimately connect with a pre-historic circle which is on the top of the hill and immediately above the terraces. I have found these lines in other places, also marking the edge of steep declivities, and therefore suggest-ing that the declivities are artificial. In another case, at Turleigh, near Winsley, Wilts, a lane leads up a cleft in the side of the valley and passes what appears to be a small quarry, with a cliff about 50ft. high, which I have always supposed to be of fairly modern construction. The track lines of the lane, however, lead off from the lane and follow the base of this cliff before returning to the existing lane, a fact which somewhat suggests that the cliff was cut away in prehistoric times so as to allow the lane to con-tinue without leaving its track lines, which otherwise, owing to the steepness of the hillside, it would have had to do.

I shall, no doubt, be asked what possible connection these track lines, even if they exist as described, can have with the prehistoric religions, and why should they become sacred, as suggest-ed ? The principal answer is that they, and the tracks, mounds, ditches, pits and stones that mark them, were boundaries. They were absolutely permanent, and no human activity could alter them. They were, therefore, the best boundaries possible, and, as I pointed out in a previous article, the ancient religions and their priesthoods, which were the real governments of prehistoric society, were much concerned with boundaries, as is shown by the known functions of Thoth, Hermes and Mercury. They have also the added advantage that they are quite hard to find, and that to do so needs a certain amount of skill which must be learned. Unless substantial quantities of water happen. to be passing under these track lines, which is unusual, the natural " village " dowser cannot, in my experience, locate them. It was therefore unlikely that uninstructed persons would discover this secret of the priests. This secret was based on a genuine natural phenomenon beyond the comprehension of the unin-structed, and therefore complied with the requirements of all good " magic."

Where, as sometimes happens, a single track line comes to an end, I have always found that it terminates in a spiral in which all its nine component lines lead to one focal point. In a future article I hope to deal with spirals, which had a great, but as yet unexplained, significance in the prehistoric religions. Beautifully executed carvings of " S " spirals on bone objects have been found near the Pyrenees, the date of which cannot be less than 10,000 B.C., and many examples are found on megalithic monuments in this country, of which the supposed date is about 2,000 B.C.

I cannot deal fully with spirals here, but should like to mention, so that others can test my statements, that at Stonehenge 18 great spirals converge on a focal point marked by the Altar Stone ; and that at Avebury the central stone in the south Circle is the focal point of twelve spirals ; and that at Stanton Drew the Great Circle of stones is aligned on a spiral which leads from the Avenue and makes an almost complete circle in an anti-clockwise direction.

There is one thing which I have noticed in the course of my investigations into these things, and that is the extraordinary preservative and self-preservative power of grass turf. Once there is enough soil for it to live on and the roots have become matted together it becomes a living and self-reproducing carpet, like the skin of an animal. It does not appear to increase in thickness unless there is some nearby source of dust such as a road, and does not die out, however little there is. Some of the turf on chalk uplands is less than two inches thick, and yet it must have been there since the end of the last Ice Age, about 10,000 years ago.

A good instance of its preservative power is in the great artificial mound known as Silbury Hill, near Avebury. This must have been constructed at least 3,000 years ago. It is 130ft. high and has steep sides, and yet, apparently because of its grass covering, it has retained approximately its original shape, including a series of terraces which encircle the top. Dowsing indicates also that its base, which covers five acres, is still within a few feet of its original margins. I was sorry to notice that the turf is now falling away in places, which I suppose is due to modern dustless roads or possibly to rabbits.

Another instance is The Cursus, a great rectangular enclosure near Stonehenge, one-and-a-half miles long. It is over 3,500 years old, but its enclosing mounds and ditches are still clearly visible. Much has been talked by scientists about erosion, and I have seen lists purporting to show the exact rate of it. These instances, however, seem to me to show that where turf exists there is almost none at all.

# SPIRALS

*Guy Underwood*

The subject of spirals has engaged the attention of thinking man ever since he became able to use that faculty and acquired the leisure to exercise it.

There is a beauty and mystery about the spiral, possibly due to the fact that it is a natural form associated with growth. Many shells are spirals, and few people can have failed to wonder at the beauty of young plants which exhibit spiral form; for example, the bracken. There is an infinity of examples.

The ancient religions were fertility cults, and the spiral has been associated with them for vast periods.

It is an interesting fact that Leonardo da Vinci made a study of them. A number of his drawings at Windsor Castle are studies of spiral forms. These include illustrations of effects produced by the disturbance of liquids; dust clouds caused by falling masonry; the patterns made by smoke; and spiral forms of plant life.

This article is not strictly confined to spirals, but relates to certain linear distortions of some unidentified condition of the earth's surface, presumably electrical, which frequently exhibit spiral form.

I propose first to make as clear as possible what I have found, and to name my offspring; secondly, to show patterns made by the ancients which bear a singular resemblance to those made by track lines; and, finally, to give as concrete examples the dowsing influences found at our most famous national monument—Stonehenge.

The most common patterns made by track lines are shown in Fig I; A, B and C being the most characteristic spiral forms.

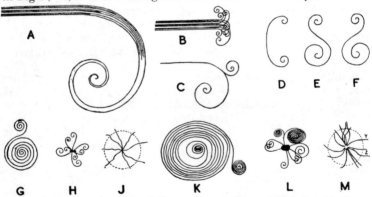

Fig. 1.—Patterns made by influence lines and perceptible by dowsing.

B shows a track line interrupted as previously described by another, and presumably stronger, crossing influence, and taking a form not unlike a much-worn paintbrush. I call this type a " brush spiral."

I call the nine individual lines, shown in A and B, of which all track lines are composed, " hair lines," and the three sets of three hair lines I call " cord lines." The whole line of nine hair lines I usually call a " track line," and where, as is frequently the case, they run in parallel pairs I call them, if necessary to distinguish them from others, " double track lines."

A is, I think, the form of simple spiral which was of most significance to the ancients. In this form the track line makes a logarithmic spiral, as a whole, without splitting up. I call it a " close spiral." There are many barrows or standing stones marking spots where these occur.

In some cases single spirals of this type, if of great size, were regarded as important. Merlin's Mount, the great tumulus in the grounds of Marlborough College, marks a vast spiral of this kind. It has at least seven, and possibly several more, whorls. The spiral path leading up and around the mound still follows approximately the course of this spiral, but the top and centre of the mound is covered by a reservoir. Dowsing suggests that this mound is a prehistoric sacred artificial mountain somewhat similar to the ziggurats of Chaldea.

This type of spiral is, however, of the greatest sanctity and importance when a number of them converge on the same focal point, as in rare cases they do. At such spots the ancients erected their temples. Such spirals are found at Stonehenge, Fig. 5, and at Avebury ; also at Silbury Hill and at certain large barrows which were really hill temples and not intended as burial mounds. The great barrow (No. 40) in Fargo Wood, Stonehenge, near the main road, and called by Colt Hoare " The Monarch of the Plain," is a good example. It has six such spirals. Several excavations have been made but no burial found. See also Barrow No. 28, Fig. 9.

D, E and F show small spirals, usually four to ten feet in length, and frequently met with. In the neighbourhood of important sacred sites the positions of these are often marked by shallow pits or hummocks. Pits marking about 30 of these are to be found within the circles of Windmill Hill. These pits have never been explained, although often commented upon.

On the down S.W. of Stonehenge, and west of the barrows shown in Fig. 8, and near the site of a former military camp, there are many small circular mounds marking these small spirals.

E is a right-hand S spiral and F a left-hand—which is to say that as the dowser approaches the focal point of E he is continually turning to his right. F is *vice versa*.

In describing spirals as right or left handed I use the same method as the conchologists. They, however, call them dexiotropic and leiotropic! The only book which I have been able to find dealing generally with spirals (*Spirals in Art and Nature*, by T. A. Cook) adopts the opposite nomenclature, as he bases the spiral on the screw, which seems to me to be a different thing. A right-handed screw is one which is easy to insert with a screw-driver held in the right hand, and goes in the opposite direction to the conchologist's right-handed spiral.

One end of an S spiral is usually larger and more complex than the other, and when marked by a pit or mound the smaller end usually lies outside, without any visible indication of its position. C spirals of the shape shown in Fig. 1 D are usually completely covered by the mounds marking them, which are frequently oval. These small spirals appear to consist of three hair lines only. They were not, I think, regarded as of great importance unless they formed a pattern or circle, as at the South Station and Hele Stone at Stonehenge. See Fig. 5 and on barrows as in Fig. 9.

Fig. 1 G shows a complex S spiral, that is to say, one in which the whorls make several turns before arriving at the focal point. I have found several of these with 8 to 12 turns at the large end. These were of considerable sanctity, and it is usually this kind which are marked by pits, mounds or stones. Large ones are often marked by barrows. See Fig. 9, No. 33. Good examples of these spirals are seen in the South Station at Stonehenge, and one marked by stone No. 23 in The Avenue at Avebury, see Fig. 1 K. These spirals are sometimes of great size, the largest I have found being 900ft. in length.

Fig. 1 H shows a typical " Octopus " symbol. I call them this owing to their shape. I have found them with four to eight radii. Their centres are always on the centre line of a track line and they are clearly associated with them. The radii consist each of a single hair line, and they differ in this respect from the somewhat similar " blind springs." They are rare and appear to have been of great sanctity. I have found none at Stonehenge, 17 at Avebury and two elsewhere. Fig. 1 L is an actual example marked by stone No. 34 in the Avenue, Avebury.

Fig. 1 J is a typical blind spring. Actual examples are shown at M and in Figs. 5 and 9. It is at the intersecting or radial point of these that burials of the late Stone and Early Bronze Ages (2,250-1,700 B.C.) were made, and possibly some later. The radii can be either underground streams or track lines, and they connect the barrow with other barrows or with some other neighbouring sacred site. The effect is that all barrows and other nearby sacred sites are connected together by a network of influence lines, with the barrows at the intersections.

# PREHISTORIC SCULPTURE

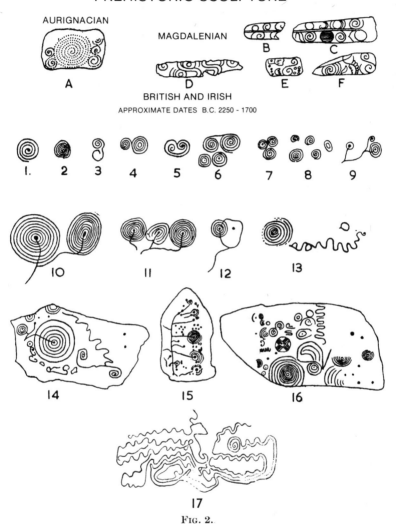

AURIGNACIAN

MAGDALENIAN

B    C

A    D    E    F

BRITISH AND IRISH

APPROXIMATE DATES B.C. 2250 - 1700

1.   2   3   4   5   6   7   8   9

10   11   12   13

14   15   16

17

Fig. 2.

## CIRCULAR TRACK LINES

Track lines sometimes take completely circular courses. It is on these that the ditches and mounds surrounding prehistoric temples are aligned. The lack of symmetry of the great circle at Avebury is due to this cause.

It was at places where "interruptions" in these track lines occur (see *B.S.D.J.* VIII, 60, p. 26) and "brush spirals" (Fig.

1 B) that all causeways across such ditches were made; see "Stonehenge," Fig. 5. Causeways were not, however, always made at interruptions—at Woodhenge there are a number of interruptions, but only one causeway. This ditch may, however, have been part of a processional way. See Fig. 10 C.

### PREHISTORIC ART

The prehistoric carvings in Fig. 2 show resemblances to some of the patterns which I have described.

Fig. 2 A is the earliest example known to me of a carved spiral. It was made by punching holes in stone and was found in Siberia with associations which indicate that it is of the Aurignacian Period (85,000 to 50,000 B.C.), that is to say that it is at least 50,000 years old.

Figs. B to F are carvings on bone of the Magdalenian period (35,000 to 10,000 B.C.). They were found in caves at Arudy, and other places, near Pau in the Pyrenees. They are usually called ceremonial wands, spear heads or spear sheaths, but we do not know their actual purpose. I should suppose that they had a religious significance. In remote parts of Wales patterns much resembling B and C are still drawn on hearth stones, doorsteps and byres "to mislead evil spirits," (see *Country Life* May 7th and June 18th, 1948).

Fig. 2, 1-16 are all sculptures on British or Irish stone monuments. I have found influence lines taking all the forms shown in 1-8, except No. 5.

With regard to 9-16 much speculation has taken place as to the meaning of the concentric rings. These frequently have a line leading out of the centre and connecting them to other rings. It has been suggested that they are plans of towns and that the lines represent tracks. They certainly have the appearance of plans—particularly No. 15. In the great cave at Niaux, near Tarascon, many drawings of the cave men have been found. These include what appears to be a plan of the chambers and passages. In the megalithic tomb of Bryn Celli Ddu in Anglesea two stones were found on which was sculptured what appears to be an elaborate plan or labyrinth (see later). This includes a spiral of four whorls, and an interesting feature is that the great majority of the incised lines are in parallel pairs similar to double track lines, see Fig. 2, 17.

As to the concentric circles it would seem that they are as likely to represent barrows as towns. In stone country, barrows are built of flat stones laid in layers, making a cone-shaped mound consisting of a series of hollow cones overlaying each other. The bottom stones of each layer would make a plan very similar to these concentric rings. If they are barrows, then the line emerging from the centre is likely to represent an influence line connecting the barrow to a nearby sacred site. In stonebuilt burial mounds the positions of radiating influence lines are marked by stones set vertically.

As to Nos. 13, 14 and 16, the wavy lines are very similar to drawings of the courses of underground streams or track lines such as are found in what are presumably geologically contorted areas.  It will be noticed that with the supposed plans there also appear spirals similar to those in my surveys.  See also Figs. 8 and 9.

FIG. 3.—Prehistoric symbols

The early religion and culture of this country is supposed to have been derived from the Near East.  Fig. 3 shows some religious symbols from that region.

Fig. 3 A.  The Red Crown of Lower Egypt.  Originally the head-dress of the Libyan " mother goddess " Neith.*  The earliest known representation of it is on pottery of about 4,000 B.C. see Fig. 3 B.  (G. A. Wainwright.  *Journal of Egyptian Archaeology*, IX, 26).

Fig. 3 C.  The magic wand of Hathor, the Egyptian goddess.  It was known as " The Great Magician."  Its powers were of lifegiving and of opening, and it was associated with birth and resurrection :  see *Evolution of the Dragon* ;  Elliott Smith, p. 190.  Griffiths, in *Hieroglyphics*, p. 60, compares it with the form shown at D (to which he attributes a biological significance) and states that it appears in that form in a representation of Osiris.

Fig. 3 E appears on the tabernacle of Min, one of the earliest of the Egyptian fertility gods (*Koptos* ;  Flinders Petrie).

Fig. 3 F shows pottery of the predynastic period, covered with spirals apparently intended for decoration.  If so, this is the earliest application of the spiral to purely decorative purposes known to me.  They may, however, have been intended for religious use.

Fig. 3 G shows a Sumerian reed pillar used at doorways and cattle byres.  They sometimes appear as at H and J on taber-

---

* One of the similarities of prehistoric religions throughout the world is that their earliest deity in human form was usually a female—known as the " mother goddess."  Hathor was the mother goddess of the Egyptians ; Aphrodite of the Greeks, and so on.  The octopus was sacred to both.  Other similarities were that they included worship of the Serpent ; with whom was associated a great deluge ; and who is associated with water generally ; mountains and caves were sacred and there was a belief in life after death.

nacles. Fig 3 K is a sacred knot from Erech. Others have been found at Mycenae and Knossos. G. R. Levy in *The Gate of Horn*, p. 231, suggests that these were used as symbols of the presence of the mother goddess Nanna of Sumeria.

Fig. 3 M shows the Lituus of the Roman Augurs, the symbol of supreme pontifical authority. Cicero in *De Divinatione*, XVII, states that the lituus of the Augurs " is the very one, indeed, with which Romulus marked out the quarter for taking observations when he founded the city of Rome." He describes it as a " crooked wand." It appears on a number of engraved gems, and these show it to have been a twig, torn from a larger branch, rather than a " stick " cut from a tree. The original rod used by Romulus was preserved in the Temple of the Salii on the Palatine Hill for several hundred years, and survived the burning of the temple by the Gauls, but was ultimately destroyed or lost. It appears in Greece on libation vessels ( *Archaelogia*, XIV, 1821, p. 386).

Fig. 3 N is the Octopus as shown on Greek embossed gold rosettes of about 1,600 B.C., and on early Greek coins.

Fig. 3 P is a religious ground drawing of the Australian Bushmen, who are still in the Stone Age ; see *Northern Tribes of Central Australia* : Spencer and Gillen. These people are believed by some authorities to have retained, largely intact, the religion and culture of remote ages. Their skulls have about the same brain capacity as that of the Piltdown man who lived about a million years ago ; see *Life in Ancient Britain* : Ault, p. 4. They say that the sinuous lines represent the wanderings of their god, and the concentric circles the places where he rested.

Fig 3 R shows the " Owl Pot " or " Mother Pot." These have been found at Troy, Cyprus, Mycenae and other places. Elliott Smith contends that this form of pot is a representation of the octopus and therefore of the mother goddess through her symbol. If this can be accepted, it follows that the " pickaxe" or " eyebrow " symbol, Fig. 3 S, which is found throughout the world, also represents the mother goddess. The symbol appears in India, on a number of standing stones (statue menhirs) in France and the Channel Islands ; and on the Folkton Drums at the British Museum. The latter are chalk cylinders of the Early Bronze Age and were found in Yorkshire.

## STONEHENGE

Fig. 4 shows the original positions of the structures of Stonehenge. Many stones have fallen or been removed, and Fig. 5 shows it as it is now. An " Avenue " links the circle to the river Avon at West Amesbury, and its junction with the circle is seen in the N.E. corner. The stone just before the junction is called the Hele Stone. The circle has four " stations," marked N., S., N.W. and S.E. A barrow exists at S and another is reputed to have existed at N. Stones mark the N.W. and S.E. stations.

STONEHENGE ORIGINAL STRUCTURES

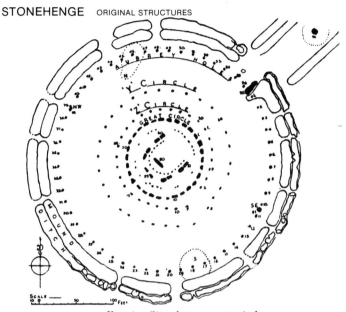

FIG. 4.—Stonehenge as erected

STONEHENGE ALIGNMENT OF CIRCLES

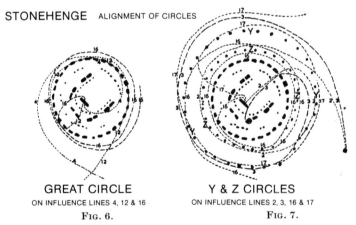

GREAT CIRCLE
ON INFLUENCE LINES 4, 12 & 16
FIG. 6.

Y & Z CIRCLES
ON INFLUENCE LINES 2, 3, 16 & 17
FIG. 7.

It will be noticed
1. That the monument is located at a spot where a large number of close spirals converge on one, or possibly two, common centres, which are covered by the Altar Stone.

89

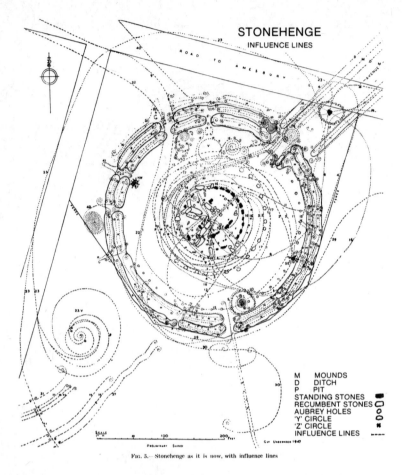

M     MOUNDS
D     DITCH
P     PIT
STANDING STONES
RECUMBENT STONES
AUBREY HOLES
'Y' CIRCLE
'Z' CIRCLE
INFLUENCE LINES   ----

Fig. 5.—Stonehenge as it is now, with influence lines

2. That the Great Circle coincides with track lines 4, 12 and 16, Fig. 6, to an extent that can hardly be due to chance.

3. That the Y and Z circles are aligned on track lines 2, 3, 16 and 17, Fig. 7.

4. That the mound and ditch follow the course of a pair of circular track lines.

5. That the Hele Stone is located on a blind spring and is surrounded by a ring of small spirals marked by a ditch.

6. That the barrows at the N. and S. stations mark the position of large S spirals, and that the South barrow has a ring of small spirals also marked by a ditch.

7. The N.W. station stone marks the position of a cluster of

small spirals, and the S.E. stone marks the termination of three important great spirals, Nos. 1, 2 and 3.

Many antiquaries have propounded that this or that part of Stonehenge is earlier or later than some other part, or that some part has been altered in position.

Dowsing suggests that all its *stone* structures were built approximately contemporaneously as integral parts of one design. The position of its structures appears to be controlled by lines of dowsing influence. If this is so, all significant influence lines must have been carefully mapped before the priests began to build, and I can see no reason why they should alter their sacred alignments. I have found no evidence that track lines alter in position. It also seems to follow that the belief that it was a Sun Temple is erroneous.

It is almost universally assumed that the Aubrey Circle is part of the original structure of the temple. It has also been suggested that it is earlier than the stone circles ; ( *Antiquity*, Vol. 3, p. 75). The principal ground for this suggestion seems to be that the Aubrey holes appear to have held wooden posts (as at Woodhenge and Arminghall) and not stones. I doubt this for two reasons ; first, because I can find no evidence that the Aubrey Circle is aligned upon dowsing influences as are all other religious structures of that period. Secondly, because, if the barrow and the holes are of a similar period, then either the barrow blots out part of the Aubrey Circle or the post holes pierce the barrow. I do not know of any other case in which one sacred structure of that period damages or partly obliterates another. Unfortunately, the question of priority cannot now be settled visually owing to careless excavation. Dowsing suggests that the barrow is earlier and that the Aubrey circle is not prehistoric, but was constructed at a time when the ancient religion had been stamped out and its structures had lost their sanctity—that is to say in the Roman period or later.

As to the wooden posts, these may have been a stockade. There are records of battles in the neighbourhood, particularly in the time of Hengist, who is reputed to have carried out a treacherous massacre there in 452 A.D.

Fig 8 shows the near neighbourhood of Stonehenge with associated barrows and track lines.

Track line T 1 is the most important, as it links the Cursus with the great circle. It enters the Great Circle between stones 20 and 21, but is not shown on the large plan in Fig. 5. Its course within the outer circle to near stone 20 is marked by vestiges of two parallel banks. This track was used as part of a lane until recent times, when the new road west of the circle enabled it to be closed. The vestiges of the banks disappear north of the centre of the circle.

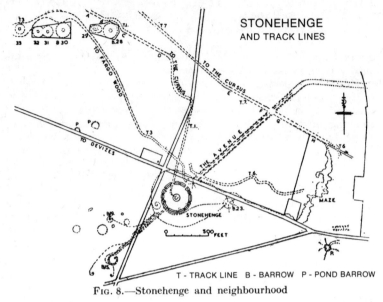

T - TRACK LINE   B - BARROW   P - POND BARROW

Fig. 8.—Stonehenge and neighbourhood

T 3 links Stonehenge to a number of barrows and to Fargo Wood.

It will be noticed that the track lines of the Avenue re-appear on the other side of the circle and terminate in spirals marked in two places by barrows.

Stonehenge is linked to the Cursus by at least two track lines. It is an interesting fact that the courses of T 1 and T 7 are each marked in two places at A-B C-D, E-F and G-H by double linear mounds, but not elsewhere, and that although these mounds are precisely in line with each other and have every appearance of being part of the same track or avenue, D and E do not connect, and the connection between B and C is indirect, and does not cross barrow No. 28 as might be supposed, but skirts it. It would be interesting to know whether air survey shows any connection between the mounds at D and E. A shepherd assured me that the intervening mounds had been ploughed away.

I have noticed in several other sites that visible indications of peculiar track line courses are misleading and apparently purposely so. To trace such courses correctly would be a good test of dowsing skill.

In Stonehenge Bottom there is a complex of winding track lines marked in the centre of the field by numerous low mounds, ditches and shallow pits. A number of influence lines forming a complicated labyrinth or maze, follow these. I traced only two of the track lines and made a rough sketch, which is shown on the plan. These mounds and pits are completely incomprehensible unless the track lines are followed.

Traditions concerning mazes, labyrinths and meanders are frequently met with, and are sometimes associated with sacred dances. Maze-like dancing grounds have remained in use all over Europe down to modern times. Here are performed what are called Troy dances. Examples in this country are at Somerton and Hilbury (Troy Towns) and some other places. It is thought to be a fertility rite. Virgil ( *Aeneid* II, 238-40) mentions a dance associated with the Wooden Horse of Troy which possibly is the origin of the dance. The Maypole dance is probably of a similar nature. In this, however, the courses taken by the dancers are controlled by the ribbons and form a pattern of a number of concentric spirals. If spirals were in fact sacred symbols such a pattern would have been of great sanctity. The sculptured stone found at Bryn Celli Ddu (Fig. 2, 17) shows what appears to be a maze.

### BARROWS

Fig. 9 shows a line of barrows N.W. of Stonehenge and near the Cursus, whose contours show up clearly on the skyline from the road. These provide a good example of the dowsing conditions existing on barrow sites and the reasons for their location and for their varying shapes.

All these, except 28 and 29, were excavated about 150 years ago by Colt Hoare, who in *Ancient Wilts*, p. 161, states that Nos. 28 and 29 were excavated by Stukeley in 1723.

No. 28 is the largest and highest of the group. It has no blind spring and is characterised by two large double spirals (4 spirals in all) meeting at the same focal point. Such a pattern was, as previously stated, of great sanctity and only excelled by other similar but more complicated symmetrical patterns. Dowsing would indicate, therefore, that it is not a burial mound. This gains some confirmation from the fact that although Colt Hoare does not state that there was no burial there he mentions none, although stating that it was excavated with No. 29, and giving particulars of finds in the latter.

In No. 29 the burial of a girl was found in the east and lower part of the barrow and two of men, one apparently early, in the west and higher end.

The double barrow, No. 29, is particularly interesting, as the two large C spirals, one inside the other, form a pattern which I have not met with elsewhere. A barrow of this shape is rare, and it would appear that its shape is due to the large spirals. It has a good blind spring in the western end and, unless I overlooked a stream, a doubtful one in the eastern. The clusters of small spirals on this and No. 31 are also unusual.

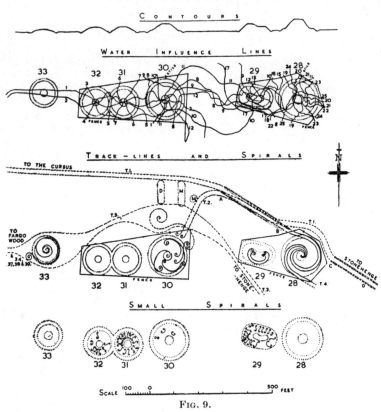

FIG. 9.

There are good blind springs, all of water reactions, under 30, 31 and 32. I did not check No. 33 for crossing influence lines.

The track lines T 1 and T 3 both lead S.E. to Stonehenge. See Figs. 8 and 9., and T 1 runs N.W. into, and continues along the mound and ditch of, The Cursus. T 3 connects with several barrows to the west and seems to finish in a blind spring on important barrow (No. 39) in Fargo Wood. Possibly it could be traced further.

The ditches of these barrows were not on influence lines. Neither have I found them associated with the ditches of other round barrows of the " bell " or " bowl " type.* I have, however, found them marking the ditches or mounds of barrows of

* " Bell '' and " bowl '' barrows are so called from their resemblance to those objects.

94

the flat type known as "disc barrows," a fact which seems to suggest the possibility that the latter are really small sacred circles, that is to say, places of worship. This has been suggested before for other reasons, see *Ancient Burial Mounds*, by L. V. Grinsell, p. 25.

It seems reasonable to assume, therefore, that the ditches of bell and bowl barrows were intended to protect the sacred mound from damage by agriculture or otherwise.

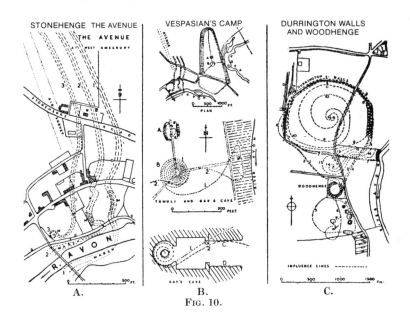

STONEHENGE THE AVENUE    VESPASIAN'S CAMP    DURRINGTON WALLS AND WOODHENGE

A.     B.     C.

Fig. 10.

Fig. 10 shows three sites which are part of the Stonehenge complex. A shows the junction of The Avenue with the Avon. Track lines 1 and 2 show the course of the Avenue as suggested by dowsing; this does not agree with the course suggested at this point by air survey. The track lines join the air survey course about 700 yards from the main road. Track line 3 joins the Cursus north of clumps of trees known as Seven Barrows. B shows Vespasian's Camp, supposed to be Roman, but which appears to be earlier. This site includes Gay's Cave, where the author of *The Beggar's Opera* wrote many of his works. This appears to be a prehistoric sacred cave. C is incomplete, but shows the connection between Durrington Walls and Wood-henge. There are at least five spirals enclosed by the Durrington Walls.

95

The courses of, and patterns made by, track lines bear a singular resemblance to lines of electrical equipotential.

As to spirals, this gains some support from the opinion of the late Dr. A. H. Church, F.R.S., of Oxford, a botanist well known for his investigations into the processes of growth of plant life. He puts forward the thesis that the logarithmic spiral curve is the ideal formula of growth and the expression of it. He also states " The distribution of living energy follows identical lines with those of electrical energy—for example, that the form of growth of shells is comparable to electrical lines of equipotential." (*Spirals in Art and Nature*, by T. A. Cook).

The tracing of influence lines on complicated sites is assisted, and, in fact, only possible, because once the dowser has picked up, and is following, one influence line, he is less sensitive to others. This fact should, I think, interest the physiologist.

For example—if following line of influence A which is crossed by B, even at a narrow angle, he will not perceive the crossing of B at all. Whereas, if he was not following another influence line he would perceive both B and A in the ordinary way on crossing them. It seems to take a few seconds to tune in to an influence line and a few seconds for it to wear off. This phenomenon provides some support for the theory that the dowsing influence involves wave motion.

It is important to keep this in mind and not to leave a track line on a complicated site while tracing it, even if a marker is put down to show the place you have left. On return you may pick up the wrong line. The best way is to carry markers with you and lay them at critical points without leaving the line until you have traced it completely : you can make any measurements needed. This selective effect only lasts for a few seconds, but usually long enough to enable the dowser, if obstructed by a bush or the like, to pick up the right line on the other side with a fair amount of certainty.

This does not mean that the dowser cannot go astray, but that, as a general rule, if he follows the influence lines in the manner I suggest, he is unlikely to do so.

It is obvious that those who wish to follow track lines must first learn to dowse. In my observation it is not hard, and is about as difficult as learning to ride a bicycle.

The usual forked twig is a clumsy indicator, and it is only those who have particularly strong reflex actions that can use it in a satisfactory manner. Its action also is slow.

It is preferable to use a " sensitive " rod. By this I mean one which will react instantly to the minute reflex movements of the normal dowser's hands caused by the dowsing influences. The most convenient form of these is the " Link " rod, and

Fig. 11 shows the best way to hold it. A makeshift can be made from two thin twigs with another short one tied to the ends with cotton, see *B.S.D.J.* VII, 58, p. 299. There are various other alternatives, such as a twig broken in two places and held together by its bark; or even a grass stem treated similarly.

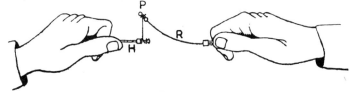

FIG. 11.

To identify and follow track lines the dowser should first practise until he can perceive the three adjacent reactions of which all water reactions are composed.* Once he can get these he should have little difficulty in perceiving the nine-fold reactions of the track lines.

The best way to follow either stream bands or track lines is to cross them with long diagonals, as this will give more time for the rod to recover between each nod. If a bend occurs it will be noticed easily.

In my surveys I have little doubt that there are many mistakes. I think, however, that they will be found to be substantially accurate. All influence lines shown have been actually traced by me. Surveys have also been made of Avebury and Stanton Drew

One object of these articles has been to put on record my observations, in the clearest possible manner, so that other practical dowsers may investigate them. I have had little time to instruct others, and, so far, almost my only supporting evidence is that of a few friends who have verified many of my statements. In several cases stones have been found on sacred sites and barrows in Wiltshire, indicating correctly the positions of important influence lines. It would appear, therefore, that one good witness is unknown to me.

Some confirmation of the existence of brush spirals and interruptions is contained in the following letter from an archæologist. He writes as follows:—

"This morning I met an old archæological friend, and mentioned to him your researches concerning barrows and Stonehenge. My friend's reply was to say that he was at Maiden Castle when

---

* Colonel K. W. Merrylees, O.B.E., was, so far as I know, the first to discover the threefold nature of the water reactions of dowsing. He called them "Trios." see *B.S.D.J.* II, 14, p. 306.

the long interior Neolithic trench was being excavated. He dowsed this trench for part of its excavated length and found that the rod indicated curves which developed. He continued, and found that after a gap more curves appeared which eventually became straight lines. He informed those in charge of the excavations that he considered there was a break in the trench, but his findings were ignored!! So that's that. Then I showed him your diagrams, and he said they exactly confirmed his findings."

# AQUASTATS
*Guy Underwood*

About two years ago a letter from Major Pogson (*B.S.D.J.*, XIII, 65) suggested that it might be interesting to attempt to trace the fissures feeding the hot springs of Bath. There are three hot springs all in the centre of the city and surrounded by blocks of buildings. It seemed pretty hopeless but ultimately I decided to attempt it.

The main spring is in the King's Bath, which is a 17th century building erected over the original prehistoric bath and spring which still exist underneath it. One day when in the Pump Room which overlooks this bath I noticed that it was empty and being cleaned, so I obtained permission to make a survey. I found a number of minor reactions but there was one strong reaction line leading from the south side to the central fountain. I traced this outside the buildings where its indicated depth was approximately 400ft. I found that although it first passed under two buildings (Woolworth's in Stall Street and a shop opposite) there was little difficulty in tracing it from there, as, after that it led me without further obstruction along various streets and out into the country in a N.W. direction and then by a circuitous route of five or six miles until ultimately it reached a hill about two and a half miles N.E. of Bath known as Little Solsbury. This hill has a triangular flat top with precipitous sides, and terraces below it near the summit.

The course of the stream, after passing along three terraces, wound about on the flat top, crossing itself time after time and becoming weaker and weaker until I lost it. In its course it followed the S.W. edge for some hundreds of yards. Other streams or branches marked most of the remainder of the edge. A number of large stones are set upright on the plateau protruding a foot or two; the stream crossed several of these so that it appeared that they marked its course and in one place the stream crossed the same stone twice. A plan of the course of the stream from Bath was duly published in the *Bath Chronicle* of April 24th, 1950.

When a stream winds about in the manner described it seems likely to be caused by a water-bearing fissure rising or falling from one stratum to another. When such a course is marked on a plan it produces a labyrinthine design similar to that produced by a piece of string dropped on a floor. I have found several such places and call them ' labyrinths.'

It seems probable to me that it is here that the main uprising of the water feeding the hot springs occurs. Geologists generally agree that the original sourse of the water of these springs is in the Mendip Hills, where the carboniferous limestone and the Old Red Sandstone stand almost vertical. From there they dip in a northerly direction reaching a depth or about two miles below the surface near Vobster, which is a depth ample to give them their heat of 120°F. The strata then rise gently and emerge in various places ten to twenty miles north of Bath.

I should mention that Bath Abbey, which adjoins the Roman Baths, is itself built over a labyrinth which may also feed the hot springs. The reactions are however weak. Another labyrinth exists under Bristol Cathedral and under the open space known as College Green opposite it. All appear to be on prehistoric sites.

The fact that the stream kept to the roads, footpaths and field divisions for practically the whole of its course was interesting and I made a survey of Bath and found that almost all the old streets had streams running lengthwise under them and that the city appeared to be underlain by a grid of waterbearing fissures running at right angles.

I also found that all the main roads (about twelve) which radiate from Bath had at least two streams one on each side usually under the pavements or the gutters. In some roads there were three or four parallel streams, the extra streams being branches of one or other of the two main streams.

Bath is remarkable for its raised pavements or " parades." There are over sixty of these, some of them ten to fifteen feet above the roads. Much of the charm of Bath is, I think, due to the fact that these parades act as plinths, which set off the buildings above them. No one has been able to explain them. Bath was largely built by speculative builders and no such builder would go to the great extra cxpense involved in erecting them merely for ornament. It would have been cheaper to cart away the earth and build on the road level as is usual. They must there-fore have been there before the houses were built. These parades occurred only where extra streams ran parallel with the main two and the side streams followed along them. All parades began where the branch stream left the main one and ceased where the branch rejoined it.

Some parades have flights of stone steps leading down to the road. They are irregularly spaced. I examined thirty-six of them and all are located at places where a branch leaves the streams on the parades and passes into or across the roadway. In most of them the visible stonework has been put there within the last hundred years or so, but I have little doubt that steps or rough stones have existed at those spots from time immemorial. Other towns have one or more similar parades with the same characteristics and there are a number of them at Clifton. These parades appear to be prehistoric walled lynchetts and many can be found in their original state in the country round Bath and have the same characteristics.

I found these things astonishing and brought to Bath all dowsing friends whom I could persuade to come, including some professional water diviners, to test them. About twelve did so and all confirmed that my plans were correct. I then made surveys elsewhere and found that these double dowsing reaction lines existed on all old roads. I have referred to them as " streams " because they give the reactions that dowsers associate with underground flowing water as distinct from metals and other reaction lines.

It will seem strange that no one has noticed these lines before. There are however I think two main reasons—(1) They have a low perceptive strength—that is to say that they do not give a strong action to the rod when crossed by the dowser and

(2) Practically all dowsing up to now has been done not as I do it—to ascertain the phenomena however small—but with the practical end in view of finding a good water supply at a convenient depth. As all water diviners are aware, there exists a multitude of minor dowsing reactions almost everywhere which either would not produce enough water, or would not do so at an economic depth, or are not due to water at all. Much of the skill therefore of the professional dowser is in my observation devoted to cutting these out and they purposely hold their rods in such a way that it will respond only to the stronger reactions. The forked twig," even if made of whalebone, is a somewhat clumsy and insensitive indicator, which is an advantage for this purpose.

I now call these double lines " Aquastats." Their characteristics are as follows :—

1. Aquastat reactions are similar to stream reactions, that is to say, that they give three definite dips to the rod with pauses between. I am not sure that they give flow lines and parallels similar to water but if they do they are at great distances difficult to check with certainty.

100

2. Aquastats run continuously without breaks. They throw off branches sometimes double like railway sidings and sometimes single. They join with other crossing aquastats and form a continuous network over the whole country wherever I have tested for them. They appear to converge on certain spots, particularly old cities, and towns, and prehistoric sacred sites. Hippisley Cox in *The Green Roads of England*, p. 5, points out that the district around Avebury appears to be a meeting place for trackways from all parts of the country.

3. Occasionally the two lines of an aquastat diverge and take separate courses. This appears to have been regarded by the ancients as important. Many old parish Churches are on prehistoric sites (see later) and I have found this phenomenon on several of them. In all cases the altar has been set either between the diverging lines or immediately opposite the divergence. Henbury Church, near Bristol, is an instance.

In rare cases the two lines of an aquastat cross each other. I have found this on burial mounds. One is at Sherrington, nearly Wylye, Wilts.

Sometimes aquastats form labyrinths. There is a good example in the churchyard at Beckington, Somerset.

4. The width of each line is two or three feet and the distance apart of the two lines varies from three to between fifty and sixty feet. The width of the roads varies with the width apart of the aquastats, except where roads have been widened. Those under four feet apart and some single branches were used to locate footpaths.

5. Aquastats produce both the positive and negative influence (see notes) and can therefore be located by any dowser whether positive or negative and either by the twig or by a sensitive rod.

6. The principal function of aquastats in the prehistoric religion appears to have been to indicate the paths along which it was ordained that man should travel. They are not found on any modern or Roman roads unless such roads happen to follow ancient courses.

GEOSTATS

In my last three articles (see *B.S.D.J.* VIII, 60, 61 and 62) I described certain lines upon which hedgemounds by roads were located and which have other interesting phenomena. I suggested that the existence of these was the cause of the winding courses of our country lanes and roads and I therefore called them " Track Lines." It is however now clear that aquastats are even more closely associated with trackways than are " track lines," and I now therefore call the latter " geostats " or " geostatic lines," in order to enable a comparison with aquastats I would like to repeat with a few additions their characteristics, which are as follows :—

1. Each geostat consists of nine reaction lines arranged in sets of three, which I call " cord " lines. Each cord line consists of three " hair " lines. The reaction is weak and consists of tremors rather than dips of the rod. To perceive them a " sensitive " rod is almost essential and I know of only two dowsers able to get them with a twig. Their average width is six to ten feet. They are always to be found one on each side of the aquastats on which the roads are aligned and the hedgemound or wall is on the centre cord line. Their distance from the aquastats is usually about equal to the width apart of the latter and it is this space which constitutes the verge of the road. Occasionally they do not keep parallel but swing away from the main aquastats so causing the otherwise often inexplicable occasional widenings of the verges of country roads. The usual cause is a side-branch of an aquastat very similar to those marked by raised pavements in towns, or like a siding on a railway.

2. Geostats appear to be secondary reactions of aquastats and to be in a state of equilibrium between two forces and in some ways much resemble electrical lines of equipotential.

3. The principal practical application of them by the ancients was as boundary lines and many of our irregular field divisions are aligned on one of a pair of geostats, the aquastats not being marked.

4. Their most important significance in the old religion was the spiral form which they assume and also that under certain rare conditions they form complete circles. In my last article the great spirals at Stonehenge and the double circle on which its ditch and mound are aligned was illustrated. These great spirals and circles appear to occur when they are completely surrounded by opposing influence lines. Such circles and large C-shaped spirals (but not S spirals) are almost always in duplicate one within the other. It is on circles of this kind that the ancients located, not only Stonehenge, but Avebury and all other similar sites that I have examined.

Very large " C " spirals appear to have had a protective significance to the ancient peoples and I have found a number of church sites enclosed within them, for example Trowbridge and Broughton Gifford, Wilts, and also some houses on very ancient sites, such as Lower Westwood Manor and Devizes Castle, Wilts.

## NOTES ON DOWSING

It is difficult to think of anything more valuable to the study of dowsing than that all competent dowsers should publish their methods and observations and the deductions which they draw from them, so that it could be seen where they agree and disagree. If they do not agree there must be some explanation which could be found by investigation.

This should lead to universal agreement on at least some basic facts which does not seem to be the case at present, and would be of immense assistance to other students.

Unfortunately most of the expert dowsers are professional diviners who are disinclined to enlarge upon the mysteries of their calling. Most of them believe that they are possessed of secrets hidden from other men, and upon which their living depends. My own feeling is that they all have the same secrets and use the same methods.

In the hope that others will follow my lead I propose to state here my own observations, conclusions and methods, which are as follows :—

I agree with most of those who have made any attempt at scientific investigation of dowsing, that the movement of the rod in the dowser's hands is due to a reflex action of his arm or hand muscles when he comes within the influence of an underground stream and that this influence involves some wave motion.

Reflex actions are due to stimulus to our nerve centres and my experiments suggest that this nerve centre is located at the base of the skull at the top of the spinal column.

If a dowser can locate an underground stream in one place clearly he can locate its course anywhere. For example : however much a stream may wind across a field he should be able and is able to mark its course. Whenever he crosses that line he is affected. It follows that what affects him is some discontinuity in the conditions, presumably electrical, of the atmosphere upon that line. Such a discontinuity is a 'line of force' and if the proposition was put to physicists in that way, instead of in the vague way in which it is generally put, I do not think it would be long before some physicist began to take a little interest, as such a line of force is at present unknown to, or unrecognized by, modern science although apparently known to the ancients.

Water by itself does not affect the dowser nor do streams rivers or other water on the surface. All that any competent water diviner claims is to locate underground streams. An underground stream can be defined as follows—Water, underground, in motion, under pressure, subject to friction and connected ultimately with the sea. So far as I am aware no dowser could pick out from a row of pots covered with a cloth the one which contained water. As to underground sewers, water adits and the like, the reaction is so slight as to be almost non-existent and few dowsers would undertake to locate and trace them, although I know of several who claim to have done so.

# DOWSING REACTIONS

The dowsing reactions are complex but can be divided broadly into two kinds—positive and negative. There are two kinds of dowser whom I distinguish as either positive or negative according to the kind of dowsing influence to which they are most sensitive. Few dowsers are equally sensitive to both.

The narrow band of influence, usually two to ten feet wide, vertically above the stream, and usually referred to as the "Stream Band," is a "positive" influence.

On each side of the stream band are broad bands of influence sometimes thirty feet or more wide. These are "negative" influences. They become weaker the farther they are from the stream band.

The effect of these two influences is as follows: Assuming that the dowser uses the ordinary forked twig and holds it in the conventional manner, that is to say with his palms upward, then as the *negative* dowser approaches the stream he will begin to feel his rod rising and the pull on the rod will become gradually stronger as he nears the stream band, where when he reaches it his rod suddenly, as he expresses it, "loses power." In other words the negative influence appears to be obliterated by the positive. Few negative dowsers are able to feel the positive influence except to the extent I have described.

The positive dowser feels practically nothing of the negative influence other than perhaps a slight kick or lift to his rod, and perhaps an almost imperceptible tingling, which warns him that a stream is near, but, when he reaches the stream band his rod will give three strong dips downward and recover with a slight pause between each.

If either kind of dowser holds his rod with palms down its movements will be reversed. It will also be less vigorous as, when held palms down, the forearm muscles are in less tension and therefore less susceptible to reflex action.

The width of the positive influence is often called the "width of the stream," but it has no relation to this. I have found no difference that I could discover between a stream known to be in a rock fissure and one known to be in gravel or sand, which may extend as a water-bearing stratum over a wide distance. Several dowsers have suggested that the influence from water-bearing strata, as distinct from fissure streams, locates itself above where the greatest amount of water flows, and that it is advantageous to use dowsing even over strata where water is certain without dowsing, as by so doing the largest and most free-flowing part of the stratum is tapped. It is however impossible to verify this. It is always, however, advisable to dowse on a chalk subsoil because although some water can be expected at a certain depth as a matter of course a far better and more permanent supply can be obtained from a fissure of which there are many and which drain away the water from large areas.

Practically all the " village dowsers " are negative dowsers or " natural " dowsers who have discovered their gift by trying the twig. They are very reliable in locating the water but can seldom estimate depth as they are usually insensitive to the positive influences by which the positive dowser ascertains depth under the " Bishop's Rule." Some, however, could do so, the best known being John Mullins, Benjamin Tompkins and Bleton, the French dowser.

I hope to deal more fully with ancient roads, barrows, church sites, barns and market crosses in a future article and trust that in the meantime other members will also make investigations.

As Mr. Underwood himself states the observations, conclusions and methods he describes are entirely his own. What he terms aquastats and geostats are found in other forms by other dowsers, e.g., Peyré (squares with circles inside), D. O. King, C. T. Gardner, and others. To associate the alignment of roads, buildings and boundaries, and the siting of ancient monuments, with the previous existence of such lines of reaction seems to be farfetched, if not fantastic. It is far more likely that the reactions described are in many cases directly due to the existence of such roads, buildings, &.., for it is well known that vertical masses and changes in density of the soil, as would occur by the making of roads and tracks, are the cause of reactions owing, probably, to the changes produced in the electromagnetic surroundings. Moreover, it is well known that reactions can be aroused by entirely subjective influences, as in map dowsing. There is no reason to suppose that our Neolithic or Bronze Age ancestors knew anything of dowsing as now practised.—EDITOR.

# AQUASTATS AND PREHISTORIC SITES
### Guy Underwood

In my last article on this subject I included some further notes on the dowsing reactions. My reason for this was to make clear all the phenomena of dowsing which I have verified by practical investigation and upon which my work on the relation between dowsing and the religion of the Stone Age is wholly based.

Some of these notes had to be omitted, owing to shortage of space, from my last article, and I am now completing them here.

### THE PARALLELS

The parallels are weak replicas of the stream band and are found on each side of it, repeating at equal distances, each reaction becoming weaker the farther they are from the stream band until they cannot be perceived further. They provide the most obvious evidence that some oscillating force is involved in the dowsing influence. They could not be produced without wave motion.

The distances apart are, on normal soils, equal to the depth of the stream below the ground, and it is by measuring this distance that the dowser finds the depth. This method is called the Bishop's rule, and has been known and practised for nearly 300 years. I know of no other satisfactory method and, according to my observations, all competent dowsers use it.

The parallels occur only with the positive reaction of the stream band. The negative reactions are not repeated at the parallels.

Many people suppose that because the inner parallels occur at an angle of 45° to the actual stream that the stream emits some " rays " or " waves " and at that angle. I know of no evidence that underground streams emit rays or waves. Such streams appear to cause a line of discontinuity in the electrical condition of the atmosphere vertically above them which is called the " stream band." The fact that the parallels repeat themselves at equal distances until they die away indicates that the primary oscillations causing them are on the surface at the stream band and do not emanate direct from the actual stream.

### " Strength " of Reactions

There are two kinds of strength of the dowsing influence, which I distinguish as " perceptive " strength and " reaction " strength.

#### Perceptive Strength

This relates to the ease with which a reaction is found by the dowser.

Some dowsing reaction lines are faint and easily missed. This occurs—
(1) Where there is a mere seepage of water
(2) In the case of streams at great depth, and
(3) In the case of the secondary reactions such as the parallels and geostats

Skill is necessary to locate and trace such influence lines. On the other hand powerful streams near the surface have strong perceptive strength, and anyone who can dowse is hardly likely to miss them. Aquastats are fairly easily located by any dowser, but their perceptive strength is not so great as a normal stream.

#### Reaction Strength

One of the most remarkable of the phenomena of dowsing is the tendency of the rod to make complete revolutions. The number of these varies with each stream or reaction and varies from about two to over seventy.

106

The number of the revolutions increases with the amount of water flowing and decreases with the depth below the surface. By multiplying the depth in feet by the number of revolutions an index figure can be obtained, and if this is multiplied by a factor increasing with the size of the index the result will give an approximate idea of the maximum quantity in gallons per hour likely to be available. See *B.S.D.J.* VI, 44 (1944).

This is the only practical method I know of estimating quantity, and I doubt whether there is a better. It cannot, however, be relied on as a definite estimate, but is a valuable guide to the dowser himself as to whether or not there is likely to be enough for the need of his client. All geologists dealing with water supplies exhibit great reluctance to give estimates of quantity, except in the vaguest terms, and all dowsers would in my opinion be wise to do the same. All that can be said for the method is that it is usually about right within a tolerance of about 20 per cent.

There is a knack in getting these revolutions which I cannot explain, but I think it lies in the ability to release completely all control of reflexes. (See Dr. J. A. Simpson Emslie, *B.S.D.J.* I, 3, p. 47, and II, 10, p. 106. After a little practice it comes naturally.

With the negative dowser the revolutions occur very shortly after he has entered and perceived the negative influence, and they become stronger the nearer he approaches the stream band. With the twig held normally they are anticlockwise viewed from the right. Negative dowsers almost all use the forked twig and by " held normally " I mean held with the palms up. If held palms down the movements are reversed.

The positive dowser should stop still as soon as he has crossed the stream band or other influence line, and the revolutions will commence almost immediately and are usually anticlockwise also. He should hold the rod lightly.

### FLOW LINES

Most mistakes in the location of streams arise from a confusion of the stream with its parallels. When I first began to investigate I had great difficulty in this and the only method I knew was to take the reaction strength of the supposed stream and of several parallels on each side until I was certain which one gave the greatest strength. This is reliable but takes a considerable time.

There is a better and almost instantaneous method for which I am indebted to Mr. George Applegate, of Trowbridge. He pointed out to me that, after crossing the stream band and on proceeding a few paces, there would be found a single (not triple) positive reaction which is peculiar to the stream band and does not occur with the parallels. What happens is as follows : If after crossing the reaction line and getting the three dips of the rod the dowser continues to hold his rod steadily, then after a few paces the rod will give first a single weak upward kick, then return to level, and then a few paces beyond will give a single and fairly strong downward nod. If it does this he can, in my experience, rely upon having found the stream. Incidentally these flow-lines are the only water reactions which are not triple.

### Tuning In

It will no doubt be asked by some readers how the course of a single reaction line can be traced in a complex of other lines as shown on my plan of the geostatic lines at Stonehenge (*B.S.D.J.* VIII, 62) or when rising fissures wind about and cross their own courses, as is not infrequent. The answer is that as soon as the dowser has picked up and begins to follow one reaction line of any kind he appears automatically to " tune in " to that line and to become insensitive to others even of the same nature. No matter how many other reaction lines may cross the one he is following, he is unlikely to be affected by any of them, although if he is careless it is quite possible to go astray. The dowser, if making a plan of a complex site, should never leave the line he is tracing until he has completed it, as otherwise on return he may pick up the wrong one.

It would be interesting to know whether this faculty of " tuning in " has any relation to the ability of fish to find their way in the ocean where they cannot see, or to the homing instinct, or even to that much discussed problem of scent in animals. It is difficult to put any construction on this phenomenon other than that some wave motion is involved, and it should be of interest to physiologists and biologists.

## OLD ROADS AND TRACKS

In my last article I described " aquastats," that is to say, dowsing influence lines which have the peculiarity of running in pairs. I pointed out that I thought the ancient peoples may have regarded these double lines as the paths along which Nature had ordained that they should travel, and accordingly they made their roads and tracks between these lines. It is this fact which explains the winding of our old lanes and roads. It also indicates that our roads are far older than one would naturally suppose and that the population of this country must have been considerably greater in the early prehistoric period than is generally estimated.

Most people have wondered why the verges of old roads sometimes widen out to two or three times the usual width and then close in again. This is due to branches or " sidings," which break away from the main aquastat and rejoin it a little farther on. See Fig. 3.

The courses of our hedgerows and other field divisions are also apparently incomprehensible owing to the winding and unpractical lines they take. It would have been easier to have made them straight, and more convenient for their purpose. The reason for this is that they also are aligned on aquastats or on water influence lines. These are usually branches from the main aquastats in the nearest road. Where this occurs the hedgerow itself is set on one of the geostatic lines (which accompany aquastats on each side) and the aquastat runs parallel with the hedgerow. I have generally found that if there is a ditch by the side of the hedgerow it is on the side along which the aquastat or the underground stream runs. Such field divisions when aligned on aquastats are really roads in embyro—approved, their proper course indicated, and ready for use if required.

What is probably the best and most convenient place for any dowser to test the statements I have made as to aquastats and geostats is on any old road or lane. One associates these with the country but there are plenty of them in any suburb, the only difference being that the suburban ones are lined with houses. The investigator should first test on an old road and then on some new road recently cut for a housing estate, &c. He will find the aquastats in the old road and none on the new. He will also be able to find the geostats at the point where the new joins the old and where the old hedge mound used to be.

The illustrations show actual examples of a section of a country lane with widened verges, field entrances and field divisions.

The letters R, L and S mean respectively that the ground levels at those places is raised above, level with, or sunk below, the land on the other side of the adjoining boundary line or fence.

It will be noticed that there is a difference in level only where an additional aquastat exists, running parallel with and near to another.

The plans reproduced above show more clearly than can be done by explanation, the manner in which roads were aligned on aquastats, and also a number of other characteristics of the ancient system.

Figure 1.—This shows a sharp bend with footpath crossing, a field entrance and aquastats running parallel with the main aquastat and on each side of it.

The field entrance is unusual, as it is on the crossing place of three aquastats instead of on one as is usual. At such a crossing

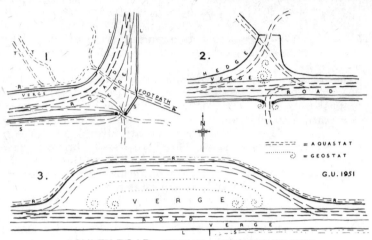

ASHLEY ROAD, WINSLEY, BRADFORD ON AVON

place I should have expected a barrow. It will be noticed that all the three aquastats branch off the same main aquastat in the road and possibly this is the reason for there being no barrow.

Figure 2.—This shows two field entrances, and a field division aligned on an aquastat. It also illustrates how a geostatic " S " spiral is often produced, that is to say, by the complete enclosure of a small space by aquastats. It will be noticed that this space is approximately equilateral.

The wave motion originating in the primary dowsing reaction lines—water and aquastats—are perpendicular to the primary line. It follows that in the example illustrated three approximately equal forces are meeting in the centre of the enclosed space and it is reasonable to suppose that the geostatic " S " spiral is a line of equipotential. The same of course applies to C spirals in enclosed spaces. (See Fig. 3). If the two aquastats running north into the fields had crossed each other at a point nearer to the main aquastat in the road the probable result would have been two " C " spirals similar to those shown in Fig. 3.

The field entrance south of the road has stone gateposts. In this part of the country this is a sure indication that they mark a place where an aquastat enters the field. Many of these posts are about two feet thick and seven or eight feet in length and weigh nearly two tons. They are in fact megaliths. No one in modern times would for economic reasons go to the trouble and expense of erecting them.

As previously described aquastats produce linear geostats which accompany them on each side and on which hedges and walls were located.

110

When a linear geostat is crossed, approximately at right angles, by another aquastat, the geostat is bisected and the two ends take spiral form as shown at the south field entrance. These small spirals are characteristic of all ancient field entrances. The linear geostats are not shown elsewhere in order to keep the plans clear.

Figure 3.—This shows a widened verge of the normal type formed by a " siding "—that is to say, a branch leaving the main aquastat and then rejoining it. The resulting breaking of the geostats between them will be noticed ; and that the concave sides are towards the shorter, and therefore presumably the weaker, of the aquastats producing them.

Readers are referred to the editorial note following Mr. Underwood's article on page 286 of *B.D.S.J.* 71. The rule for finding depth referred to by him is more suitably described as the rule of the right-angled isosceles triangle and is not necessarily associated with any system of parallels. The effects of anomalies in the sub-soil and on the surface and of vertical objects can be appreciated by any sensitive dowser, and it is reasonable to suppose that the reactions described are due to them. The reference to " ancient people " is too vague to be of any archaeological significance.—EDITOR.

## OLD CHURCHES OVER STREAMS
### W.H. Lamb

I have noticed that in old churches there are two streams of water at different depths that cross under the high altar. Had this happened once or twice one might call it coincidence, but when it is found in several cases with no exception; that surely is remarkable? I myself have observed this in every old church I have been in during the past three years, although this perhaps was no really great number. So far I have not found the exception, and one naturally asks why. We do know of course that early churches were often built over sites originally sacred to pagan worship, but did these pre-Christians worship running water, and by what method did they locate the underground stream confluence?

## OLD CHURCHES OVER STREAMS
### Muriel Langdon

I read with interest your correspondents' note on old churches over streams. A few years ago I discovered that old churches are planned on a complex system of " hidden springs " or " domes." In these I found that the component streams appeared to rise vertically and then curve over in the shape of a ' dome ' till they

111

met at its highest point.   The water then rose vertically for a bit, then divided and descended as separate streams;  again in the shape of a dome, finally falling vertically.   If a well I find is dug on a dome, the lowest depth the water reaches is the difference in height between these upper and lower domes.   To the dowser the streams appear to be like the spokes of a wheel, some flowing inwards to the hub and some outwards.   These domes are mostly very small streams and can be easy to miss unless one is looking for them.   I found my first quite by accident.   They mostly occur in groups along straight lines, but may be on a circle too, though this is rare.

Now old churches appear to have been planned on the lines of these domes.   A line runs up the centre of the nave and chancel and another across from the north to the south doors.   The altar I find is always on a dome, as is also the centre of the chancel steps, the font and all doors.   These domes are quite separate from each other owing to the fact that the water rises and plunges vertically a few feet from the centre of the dome.

Some odd planning is thus explained: for instance nave and chancel not aligned, and doors in curious places;   St. Peters, Rome and the cathedral at Florence show where these little streams flow in the patterns of their lovely marble floors.

There is an association between water and religion that stretches back to a remote past.  The siting of the stones of Stonehenge*; Avesbury, and Arbor Low is completely explained by the water patterns.   Barrows too are sited on these hidden springs.

This association seems to have been broken in very early Christian times, as the primitive little Welsh churches are not connected at all with a water pattern.   These I find, by dowsing to be an integral part of Romano-British settlements.   To find out when the custom started again would make interesting research.

(*Confirmed and exhaustively surveyed by Guy Underwood as reported in B.S.D.Js. 58-61 December, 1947 to September, 1948 " Archaeology and Dowsing.")—Ed.

# THE MOULTON DOWSE
## P. Leonard

This is a condensed summary of a dowse which I have in progress.   I call it a dowse in progress because, from what has turned up to date and from the past time factor involved, it will probably take many years to complete.

In May, 1977, I was shown a print of a 16th century map of Northamptonshire.   This map shows that our village of Moulton had a castle, which the owner of the map advised was about 13th century according to his information.

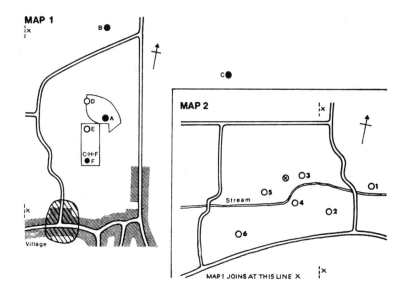

MAP 1

MAP 2

Stream

MAP 1 JOINS AT THIS LINE X

Village

Later in May, during conversation with a friend who is also chairman of our local parish council, I told him about the map and " Moulton Castle." His reaction, naturally I suppose, was to think it might be a great idea to see if it was possible to find the site or any remains of the castle, as it would be good for the history of the village.

About a week later he asked, if through any type of dowsing, I could give any pointers to the castle site. Thinking over the problem, I decided that the best way to tackle it would be:—
1. An initial map dowse.
2. Followed by a mental dowse of whatever area showed up.
3. Followed by a time dowse.
4. Followed by an actual site dowse.

A day or two after this my friend who owned the map advised that a field about a mile away was called " Castle Hill field." This seemed a good pointer to where to commence a map dowse. (See Map 1, C.H.F.). Using the area surrounded by the roads, and using the roads as a border to dowse within, I commenced a map dowse, seeking a site of habitation in the past. I made what has proved to be a fortunate error by forgetting to state how far back in time I wished to dowse. The pendulum gave me site A, which subsequently I found was boggy ground in the middle of a wooded scrub area, on the south side of a slope. As so often happens when map dowsing, the pendulum wandered off and gave sites B and C.

113

On 13th June I carried out a mental dowse of the area, still using the roads as a border to work within. Of the 48 answers that came up the following have sufficient evidence to date to at least partly confirm them.

1. That the castle building was erected on the flat.
2. That the building was generally round.
3. That the building was 75ft. in diameter.
4. That the reputed John FitzJohn was the local squire at the time of building.
5. That John FitzJohn spent more time away from this area than he spent there.
6. That people had possibly been buried within the area of the castle.

A time dowse of the area gave the building as being erected in 1284 to 1287 and *finally* pulled down about 1479.

The evidence to date which supports these answers is as follows:

In the early part of June, shortly after completing the mental dowse, the chairman and I visited site A and found it as previously described. We walked to the top of the slope and found that it was, in a sense, the shape of a mountain with a flat top. From this top there was 360° vision, the shortest vision distance being about 1 mile, the farthest vision distance being about 3-4 miles— ideal for a castle site. The flat top supports answer 1. It was 24 paces in diameter, which corresponds to answer 3, and more or less circular, as stated in answer 2. A dowse of the top indicated two lots of bones about 10ft. down, and burials were indicated in answer 6. This is site D on the map.

A little later in June the chairman obtained photostat copies of records from Delapre Abbey, our local records office. These records state that the village is 11th century. They speak of an artificial elevation, which may have been the site of John Fitz-John's castle, which when worked out from its location with known past buildings ties up with the mound mentioned. It also states that John FitzJohn was the lord of the manors of Moulton and Lincoln (see answers 4 and 5). Lincoln being no doubt the larger area, he would have required to spend more time there. The only date mentioned in connection with John FitzJohn is 1276, which is 8 years earlier than the building date discovered by my time dowse.

During July we heard that the field known as Castle Hill field had over many years during ploughing turned up " dressed stone " in odd places. As there was a crop of barley on the field at that time we naturally could not walk the area until after harvest. It was September before we finally got on to the field. In the meantime I carried out a " mental search " to see if the area had been inhabited at all and a " time dowse " for the dates of habitation.

The mental search gave a definite " yes " to habitation, with a total of 24 people on site as the largest number. The number of buildings came out as 5 and these were located as shown on Map 2. The answer to the question of a burial was yes. The time search gave the period of habitation, using our present day calendar, as from afternoon 23rd September, A.D. 843 to evening 28th December, A.D. 1150.

On Sunday, 25th September, I arrived at the field at 6.30 a.m. and carried out a site dowse, using the left hand, to search the area. In order to save a lot of walking when covering a large area I use a technique of searching with the left hand, palm facing outwards, with a mental switch to whatever I am seeking in general.

The " feel " of the hand gave three initial points of interest which I traced down. At each point I reverted to the willow fork, my personal favourite, as I am more in sympathy with willow than with any other substance. I used the fork vertically to pivot rather than horizontally to pull, as this is far more sensitive.

Dowsing for " stone handled by man in the use of his buildings or shelter," at the first dig of a hole 6ft. x 2ft. x 3ft., I obtained one piece of stone. At the second hole, about 15ft. away, I dug about 2ft. square and 6-8in. deep and came up with two smaller stones, still of the dressed type. At the third hole I came upon a floor about 14in. down, which when opened out measured approximately 7ft. x 10ft. (Site E on Map 3). The chairman and I took about 15 hours to carefully dig out this floor. From amongst the stones of the floor I brushed out a few small pieces of pottery and some bones.

At this stage the chairman arranged for the Northampton Archaeological Department to visit the site and appraise the pottery. From their detailed examination the pottery has been pronounced as 10th and 11th century and some pieces known as " Stamford Fine." The floor has been dated as Pre-Conquest, i.e. before the Norman invasion, and about 8th to 9th century with a fair amount of certainty. So, what with the floor and the pottery on this one spot alone, the " time dowse " is fairly accurate. The floor has now been officially logged with the County records and is considered of extreme importance, as so little evidence is left of mankind in the area from Roman times up to the 16th century.

About 30 yards away from the floor I got a bone response. This I am fairly sure will be proved out as the burial of a female who died at 13 years 7 months of age.

Our chairman, who is getting fairly good with a pair of angle rods, found an " interesting spot " 45ft. from the floor. This was dug out and we found partial remains of a broken pot, which we are now waiting to have dated.

It is possible that this site is going to have a preservation order

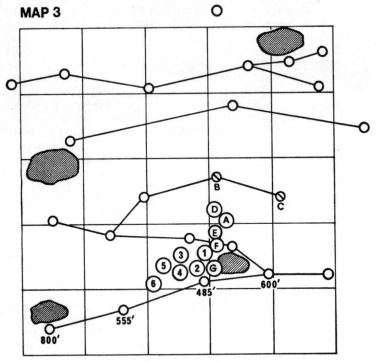

**MAP 3**

O.S. Map    Sheet SP 76 NE. 6in. to 1 mile.

O - - -    Points of earth's natural concentration of energy.

           Old parts of present day villages.

1 to 6.      Neolithic Moulton.

A to G     Sites as described.

placed on it. Also, if funds allow, the Archaeological Department will carry out a complete dig in about 5 years' time. This dowse has extended the known history of the parish back by 200 years.

I will now go back one week to Sunday, 18th September, as it becomes relevant in that order. On that Sunday evening we had our first walk on the field to see if anything of interest was to be found. There were many bits of pottery lying on the surface, some of which we collected. The chairman's young son found a stone which appeared unusual and interesting. All these items were handed to a local archaeologist on the Monday to see what she made of them. On the Sunday night I decided to explore on the map sites A, B and C. All three sites proved out as habitation sites. The time dowse gave A as 13,600-13,850 B.C., going backwards in time; B was approximately 25,000 B.C. and C approximately 20,000 B.C.

On the evening of Wednesday, 21st September, we had a meeting with our local archaeologist to see what she made of our bits and pieces. The pottery was a mixture of 11th and 18th century, and we were advised that this could be fairly normal on agricultural land, as pottery gets taken out with the dung over many years. As to the interesting stone, this was possibly a Neolithic stone scraper, which our archaeological friend said was not in keeping with the area. Yet a few days previously the time dowse of site A, which is only about 200 yards away, came within Neolithic times (10-15,000 B.C.). As to sites B and C, these came *exactly* on the spots of two local points of the earth's natural concentration of energy. I will return to this subject later.

On Sunday, 9th October, we visited site C at 10 a.m. At the exact position shown on the map, there in the field we found a natural " half bowl " shape in the side of the slope of the field. At the front edge of the half bowl three streams intercross, one above the other, at depths of 20ft., 42ft. and 63ft. Whether this is the " natural concentration of energy " I am not sure at this stage. Walking the site with 20,000 B.C. man in mind, I have no doubt that this was inhabited then. When time allows I will explore this area more thoroughly. Site B we haven't yet had time to see.

Now there are two essential factors common to sites E, A and C.
1. Each site is on the southwest side of a slope, which would give shelter from prevailing north-easterly winter winds.
2. All sites are within about 200yds. of natural streams.

So it would appear that the sites were not settled haphazardly but that careful thought went into the choice of location.

About a week ago I was advised that some years ago a local resident found some British-Romano coins and flint arrow heads in a field to the west of the village. I carried out a map dowse within the area of Map 2 to see if there were any traces of Roman habitation. Nothing has responded so far. I then switched to habitation by Neolithic man and came up with the sites marked. One comes just outside the boundary. A mental search gave 7 families inhabitating the 6 sites of Neolithic Moulton. A time dowse gave overall approximate years of from 13,700 to 14,900 B.C. These sites also have the common factors of being near a natural stream and of being sheltered by higher ground to the north of them.

Returning to the points of the earth's natural concentration of energy, Map 3 shows 23 points over a 2 mile square area. Three of the points come just outside the border. The map dowse for these I did some four months ago. I used the same map for

117

dowsing as previously described. The interconnecting lines flow from west to east. They also follow a natural rise and fall cycle of nature. I have mentally depthed the bottom four points, which you will see also follow the natural rise and fall pattern. A mental search of all points gives only the *possibility* of some type of electrical energy or force at about .75 of a volt. This is investigation for the future. Maybe someone can shed a little light from his own experience.

Now sites B and C are both exactly on points, not *near* but exactly. All other sites, even to modern day villages, fall between or close to, the lines. Somewhere between 20,000 B.C. (site C) and 15,000 B.C. (site A) mankind changed in some way, in that they lived between the lines, yet still chose their sites with care.

Did man before 20,000 B.C. consciously seek out these points, as he could recognise and use the energy? Or did he subconsciously seek the points without knowing? Why has he moved away from these exact points after 20,000 B.C.? Did he mentally and physically change, so that he had less use for them? Was it in any way harder to live on the points, so that mankind sought a little harmony in between? Site A is almost midway between two lines. Sites 1-5 are also about midway, yet the people who lived there also have sought shelter and water.

The modern day extensions of all four villages now stretch right across the lines, but I think we can put this down to boundary and social pressures owing to the increase in population and to financial considerations.

Could these points have any connection with early ley lines, even though they don't run very straight? If so, why are only two points inhabited? The question also arises of how long these points and lines have been in existence. When I map dowsed these I had no thought of ley lines in mind, just " earth's natural energy." So you can see how my fortunate error on the first dowse comes in.

It would also appear to show how civilisation is interlinked, because what started out as a search for a castle has, through links of time, connected back as far as 25,000 B.C., provided that my time dowsing turns out as accurate as my floor and pottery.

Since writing my first report (see Journal 181) I have dug a pilot hole on the edge of the flat top of the "castle site." It would appear that the flat top *may* be covered with a layer of a mixture of clay and small sandstone, with a layer of small sandstone on top of this; obviously, a good solid base to build on. We intend to excavate the " castle site " in the summer of 1978.

Two other items, which I didn't include initially, as I didn't think they were of sufficient interest, have now become a little more important.

1.  On Map 2 the X in a circle is a point which I initially map dowsed for the likelihood of neolithic tools. Three weeks ago, and about 30ft. away to the left of this mark, I found a neolithic hand hammer as used in chipping flint, also a pointed auger which they used for making holes in skins before sewing them together. From the amount of broken flint that turned up after the field had been ploughed it would seem that I have found their flint bed source. I have another map mark which came in the field near site 3, but as yet the field hasn't been ploughed and the weather hasn't been fit for walking the land.

2.  See Map 1—the hatched area. Around June or July, 1977 I was doing a mental search of the village to see where the village centre had moved to over the years. I worked only as far back as the B.C. time line. At that time line the village centre was as approximately shown. This didn't seem at all important until site F came up, just after Christmas, 1977.

You will note that sites B, D, E, F and G all fall on approximately the south to north line, too close to the line for mere chance. Did magnetism lead mankind to build so close to this line? Are there greater powers along this line, that have affected him more than he realises? Is it part of a ley line? At this stage the questions are endless, the answers yet to be found.

Site F completes this 1977 dowse.

Just before Christmas the chairman of our local council remarked that we hadn't found any complete artifacts in our search during the year. Lying in bed on Boxing Night I remembered his remark, and decided to do a mental search there and then.

Now it depends on what connotation the subconscious puts on the word " artifact," so I decided I would give my subconscious a free hand to find an artifact complete, and programmed it as follows:—

1.  Search within the parish boundary.
2.  To find an artifact complete.
3.  It must be in an area where it can be dug out.
4.  Preferably it shouldn't be deeper than 6ft.

After what seemed to be about 5 minutes I got a ready response. Doing a compass search for the wavelength which the subconscious had selected, I finally tracked it down to the southern end of Castle Hill field. I asked the subconscious to work it out in my paces from the west hedge and the south hedge. This came out as 48 paces from the west hedge and 16 paces from the south hedge. A depth search gave 2ft. 7in.

On the morning of 28th December, 1977 I went to the field and paced out 48 x 16 as indicated, and dug a hole about 3ft. square. At approximately 2½ft. down I came upon stone. This stone was overlapping, as I found when I moved a few pieces. At this stage I filled back in, went to see our chairman and arranged for us

119

both to dig on the following Sunday, 1st January, 1978. On that date we arrived at the field at 9.45 a.m. and between us dug out a hole about 10ft. square and eventually 6ft. deep, to the bottom layer of a wall. How far this wall extends we don't know, as further excavations are now necessary. There are 6 courses of stone, all overlapping. None of the stone shows any sign of being dressed in any way. There aren't even tool marks, so it would appear that the stone had been knocked together or smashed down to break it. At about one o'clock we fetched our friend the local archaeologist to look at the find. She couldn't place it in any particular period, as it was unlike anything she had ever seen before. Photographs which she took were developed and submitted to the Northampton Archaeological Society for recognition. On the Sunday evening I tried a mental search of the site when back home in bed. The only information I could get was a time dowse of B.C. 16,494—16,767, but I couldn't get a definite yes to habitation.

Looking at my map next day, I noticed that this site F was exactly on a line between two points of earth's energy and approximately halfway between (See Map 3—site F). I am faced with two possibilities regarding the lack of information.
1. Is the fault within me? To a certain extent I go mentally passive at the same time as the plants do at the beginning of their winter rest. Last year plants went passive on 3rd October.
2. Is the linking line between the 2 points of earth's natural energy locking in the information wavelengths? If this is so, why was I able to ascertain the time wavelength with relative ease? Although at the moment this is just a personal thought, with nothing to substantiate it, I wonder whether " Time wavelengths " will be found to be unique, quite unlike any other wavelength that mankind will recognise. Could the time wavelength permit future space travel in generations to come? My apologies for digressing a little.

On 4th January, 1978 our chairman had a telephone call from Mr. Glen Ford of the Northampton Archaeological Department. He said that nobody in his department could recognise or make sense of the photographs of the wall; it was new to them. He also suggested that I should pack up, otherwise I might destroy evidence through lack of knowledge of the various sites. They are not prepared at this stage to come in with us. I suppose, like many people, they think my finds are pure chance or luck. To date I have only advised them of one neolithic site. I have 8 yet to declare. However, our local archaeological friend is only too pleased to get our bits of pottery and flint finds appraised. Maybe I should wave the fact of 8 further sites in order to get quicker confirmation.

My total for 1977 is 13 sites, one of which is tools, and 23 sites of earth's natural energy. Concerning natural energy, it is becoming clearer that this is of a low frequency or wavelength, still with about .75 of a volt involved.